# COMPASSION FOR PETS

## DR. R. GEOFFREY BRODERICK

### Veterinarian and Veterinary Nutritionist

Published by:

dragon
treebooks

1620 SW 5TH Avenue

Pompano Beach, FL 33060

Cover design by Vincent Kelly

Interior illustrations by Sandra Lewis

Printed in the United States of America

ISBN (Hardcover): 978-0-9977478-2-9

ISBN (Ebook): 978-0-9974513-3-7

Library of Congress Control Number: 2016946687

For more information, please visit

www.dragontreebooks.com

"Let food by thy medicine and medicine be thy food."

"Make a habit of two things: to help;

or at least to do no harm."

—HIPPOCRATES OF KOS (C. 460 BC–377 BC)

# TABLE OF CONTENTS

# DEDICATIONS

## Dr. Russell A. Frey, KSU College of Veterinary Medicine, Class of 1952

THIS BOOK IS DEDICATED TO DR. RUSSELL (RUSS) Frey, KSU 1952. The father of veterinary nutrition (1969) in the United States of America. Russ started the first class in nutrition taught in any known medical school of any kind in the United States. He was a brilliant, down-to-earth teacher, who made everything easy to understand and learn. His vast academic knowledge was easy to grasp by his common sense approach to the uncomplicated truth about nutrition. He believes as Hippocrates did: "Let food be thy medicine and medicine be thy food." Russ was our teacher and friend. When he walked into the classroom with his immaculate white wraparound lab coat and his beautiful, loving aura of his students, the room became quiet and the smiles shined on all of our faces. We listened, laughed, and learned with him, the dynamic answer to medicine that he taught us. Prevention! I was in this first class of nutrition. Why? There are no coincidences. Russ was my mentor and I became his protégée.

Everyone who knew him loved him. He remains one of the great heroes of my lifetime and as for what I have accomplished, it was because, as sung to him one night (in the presence of a full house at Kansas State University), he was the wind beneath my wings.

## Dr. Dan Upson, KSU College of
## Veterinary Medicine, Class of 1952

THIS BOOK IS ALSO DEDICATED TO DR. DAN UPSON, my professor of pharmacology at Kansas State University College of Veterinary Medicine, who shared his knowledge and profound observations with us (the class of '69) in and out of the classroom. He shared with us feelings and experiences that were deeply personal, as well as, profoundly academic. His unique style and down-to-earth way of teaching us, with his powerful delivery of what he (not necessarily the drug industry) believed in, gave us an insight into a man who will always be remembered as one of the greatest teachers of my lifetime.

## And

### To Angel, who, when I was three years old, set the course of my life.

# ACKNOWLEDGMENTS

YVONNE, MY LOYAL WIFE AND PARTNER FOR FIFTY-three years, encouraging me and being by my side as I reached dream after dream.

My Geoffrey, Michele, and Kristina, all of my children for their love, loyalty, and support.

My Todd, for encouraging me to write *Compassion for Pets.*

My famous FDNY father, Captain Ed Broderick, my best friend, who set a valiant example and let me become me.

My amazing mother Irene Quirk, who gave me my flair and taught me how beautiful life could be.

My aunts May, Gerti, Ann, and Loretta, and my cousins George, Maurene, and yes, my Ann, who all believed that I was chosen to become the American Dream.

My grandmother from Athlone, Ireland, Annie Ferrall and grandfather "Big Dan" Quirk, who put the telegraph across the American west.

To my brother Col. Steve Broderick, who served two and one-half years (tours) in Vietnam and was one of the most highly decorated soldiers of that war. He was the bravest man I have ever known. He epitomizes the title of hero.

My sister Lynne (Buggie), for her love and brilliant research and talent in writing the history and genealogy of my family. Because of her, I know where I came from.

Captain Bill Harwood, who taught me to fly, and that the sky was not the limit.

Joey McBride, the cowboys, and Native American members of The Gerry Partlow's Black Diamond Wild West Show, who were my high school teachers.

Allan Corey Jr., Pete Bostwick, Terance Priece, Alan Gerkins and "Uncle Joey" Rizzo, who were my teachers of polo.

Doris Hamilton, a saint with the stigmata of Jesus Christ on her hands, feet, head, and chest, for her eternal love and friendship.

Linda Clark, who first taught me about angels.

Mother Teresa, who sat with me and told me the truth about animals.

Dr. Richard Passwater, who said to me, "Geoff, you have so many great stories to tell. You have got to write a book." "But, how do I do that?" I asked. Dick replied, "Just sit down in a quiet place and write one thought at a time."

Jon VanZile, who created the tree and its branches so that my words could sprout and turn to leaves.

Johnny Forman, Brent Botes, and the creator of Dr. Geoff's.

Dr. Morty Netupske, whose answers to my requests were always the same, "OK, I'll be right there." He was a great surgeon and a beautiful man. All of Huntington should be proud to have known him.

My first client, Virginia Partrick, and all of my clients who followed and continued to share their personal knowledge, experience, and wisdom with me. You have helped me learn and unconditionally verify that being a teacher of nutrition to my clients is at least equal to any other talent that any doctor can possess.

Vincent Kelly, for the covers and for your loyalty, friendship, and trust over the past four decades.

Sandy Lewis, for the magnificent illustrations that grace every chapter of this book.

Thank you Lisa, Luann, Irene, and Lori. Every day I learn something new.

To Grace, Joy, Joanne, Bonnie, Lauren, Lech, Tomek and Felix, for your love and dedication in building Cornucopia.

Dr. Ray Heinicki, for the brilliance and patience of helping me design and manufacture pet foods that changed an industry.

Thank you Mrs. Forlano of PS155, who took a new student and saw that he could act simply by playing himself.

Lee Dellin, my first angel, my big brother Dick Dellin and Betty Kamen, who taught by example.

Drs. Bob Cathcart, Fred Klenner, Irwin Stone, Wendell Bellfield and Lyle Baker, my teachers of natural medicine.

To Dr. Bruce Levine, for sharing his years of knowledge and friendship with me.

To Jack Dreyfus (the Lion of Wall Street), for giving the world the gift of phenytoin.

To my friend and colleague, two-time Nobel Peace Prize winner Dr. Linus Pauling, who defied every medical profession in his quest to save lives and prevent disease. One young man that he helped me save was my son.

Dr. Yasmine Marca, for creating "The Master Healing Plan." I know now and understand why it took years of work to put together a naturopathic and tribal traditional healing bible.

Jeffrey M. Smith. The information in the chapter on genetically modified organisms (GMOs), was taken by me, from his groundbreaking books "Seeds of Deception" and "Genetic Roulette."

Steven M. Druker, for his step-by-step blow-by-blow, name-by-name account of how the world has been deceived since the inception of the movement to genetically modify foods, so brilliantly demonstrated in his book "Altered Genes, Twisted Truth." His references were paramount in my education on the GMO cartel.

Tom and Mable Robinson of South Ozone Park. You taught with patience and love a boy of nine the art and science of genetics and breeding champion homing pigeons. Part of that love was teaching me the fact that buying the best food possible, no matter what the cost, will produce a superior individual, whether that individual is a horse, a cat, a dog, a pigeon, or a person.

Thank you to my brothers and sisters of the Kansas State Veterinary Medical School, Class of '69 for putting up with me. I love you all.

All of you who share with me the unique and fantastic experience of being a veterinarian. We are blessed to have spent our time on earth caring for these amazing animal beings.

To Skunkie, Jack, Bambi, Madeline, Doorstep, Shardee, Casey, Cardinale, Brown Dog, Black Cat, Gretchen, Pompy, Temptation, Annie Farrel, and my first horse Brandy. To all the horses that carried me to victory in the most gallant and most dangerous sport in the world, polo.

And to all the creatures who have put their trust in my hands and my heart and allowed me to try to make a difference in their lives to relieve the harm that had come to them. We will all be together again, I promise you.

**With Blessings and Eternal Love,**
**Geoffrey "Doc" Broderick**

# FOREWORD

## by Richard A. Passwater, PhD

YOU WILL BE GLAD YOU READ THIS BOOK AND YOUR pet will be even happier and healthier! The fact that Compassion for Pets exists makes me happy too as a nutritionist because it means that Dr. Geoffrey Broderick, DVM (or simply Doc Broderick as his clients and colleagues know him) found the time to write down his wisdom about pet nutrition and health.

The result is a practical guidebook that anyone can use to emulate the outstanding pet health and clinical results Doc Broderick obtains in his practice.

Doc Broderick is a fascinating man and an outstanding vet. I have known of the amazing clinical results achieved by Doc Broderick since the mid-1970s when I chatted with him at various nutrition meetings for humans. I often found Doc Broderick at the same meetings informing people about better diets for pets. He had even developed an improved pet food that was unheard of at the time—but widely respected now—a healthy blend of natural whole-food ingredients. Doc Broderick was often an invited lecturer to discuss his clinical results with vitamin C on hip dysplasia in dogs. He was invited to lecture at human nutrition meetings because of the implication that if vitamin C had such dramatic beneficial effects in dogs, perhaps it would help human bones and joints as well. We were both invited to speak at the 1978 World Congress on Vitamin C held in Palm Springs, CA to commemorate the 50TH anniversary of the discovery of vitamin C.

The last time I had the opportunity to chat with Doc Broderick at length was in 2014 in Ocean City, MD. We spent the day mostly discussing the outstanding results Doc was obtaining in his practice with his diet recommendations that he had honed over decades of clinical experience. After several interesting hours, I finally said "Doc, you just have to get this information out to the people. Not just a scientific meeting where it can be buried in with less important studies, but directly into the hands of pet owners. Your basic principles are simple and easy to understand, but the details can be confusing to someone listening to you in your clinic. They need something in writing to refresh their memories. Even I can't remember all of the important information you have told me today. You need to put it in writing and in a form that people can use as a guide. You should write a book."

The book title *Compassion for Pets*, not only describes Doc Broderick, but I'm sure it also applies to you as well. I know it describes my nephew, Steve, and his wife,

Melanie. They have four rescue dogs as a result of falling in love with them while volunteering at a shelter. They also volunteer in shelter fund-raisers such as "dog washes" and car washes. Seeking only the best care for their dogs, they researched the subject and were led to Doc Broderick. Since we share the same lasts names, they were surprised that when they called Doc Broderick, he asked if we were related. A small world event, but my point is that the word of Doc Broderick's outstanding clinical results and quality of life of his animal patients has gotten around. Reading Compassion for Pets will explain why and tell you how to achieve similar results.

There are many things to learn from the book, but a few "take home" thoughts include:

1. Since we were children we were mislead by many people that we trusted when they told us not to

feed our human food and leftovers to our pets. This is not the truth.

2.  Why would we give our pets inferior food that we ourselves would never, ever eat?

3.  We must learn what pet food really is, where the ingredients come from and how it is made.

4.  Our four-legged children should be eating the same quality food as our two-legged ones.

5.  We will learn from this book how to read and understand the information (and deception) on a pet food label and be able to separate the marketing hype from the reality of what pet food is actually made of.

6.  We will learn the difference in the requirements of the diet of an omnivorous carnivore (the dog), and an obligate carnivore (the cat).

7.  We will learn to pay back those crucial members (one out of five in the average American family)

who have protected us, kept us warm, provided us with sanity and comfort, and have given us the gift of unconditional love.

8. It is unacceptable to lose one-half to two-thirds of a pet's life by feeding non-human-grade, toxic pet food.

These points are just an example of what can be learned from Compassion for Pets. Enjoy the reading and enjoy the better health of your pets!

**Richard A. Passwater, PhD**

**Berlin, MD, 2016**

# CHAPTER ONE

# Introduction: Feeding Healthy Animals

*If you want the pet to be part of the family,*

*feed the pet like part of the family.*

IF YOU'RE LIKE MOST PET OWNERS, YOU'VE WALKED down the aisles at your local supermarket or "big box" pet shop and been overwhelmed by the selection and variety of pet foods. There is dry food and wet food. Formulations for every conceivable type of animal:

adults, puppies and kittens, large breed and small breed dogs, "lean" food for overweight animals, and of course a bewildering universe of label claims and ingredients. Would your cat prefer duck, wild game, or fish? Is your dog the kind of dog who wants ground meat or meaty cuts of beef swimming in some type of brown gravy? Or does your pet need a prescription diet for animals with sensitive skin? Is there a real difference between "natural" and "organic" pet food and the bargain brands that come in bags the size of industrial cement? And what are "meat by-products" anyway?

I'm here to help you demystify the world of pet food and teach you everything you need to know about your pet's nutritional needs. I've devoted my professional life as a veterinarian to designing healthy food for animals. I firmly believe I was put on this earth to improve pet nutrition, and I believe my work speaks for itself.

Unhappy with the selection of commercial pet foods, and after seeing the overall poor condition of the animals and red dye passing in the stool, I developed my own natural, organic line of pet foods more than forty-seven years ago. This was long before anybody was using the word "natural" as a gimmick to promote pet food. In fact, I was one of the pioneers in the natural pet food movement. It's been a long road from those early maverick days when people thought we were crazy for working so hard on our pet food to today—when pet owners like you are actively seeking out the very best premium food for their pets.

From the beginning, my belief was that if it wasn't good enough for me to eat, it wasn't good enough for the animals that share our lives. So during my career, I've personally sampled every lot of pet food produced under my name. I know that sounds a little extreme, but my position is that pet food shouldn't be comprised of inferior, leftover ingredients from industrial and agricultural production, including discarded waste products. Instead, I believe in making human grade, organic pet food from the highest quality, most nourishing ingredients on the planet—and I have scoured the planet looking for the best ingredients to include in my pet food formulations.

Now that I've got your attention, you're probably wondering: Who is this doctor who helped pioneer natural, organic pet food and has been eating pet food for almost half a century? Why should I trust him?

My name is Dr. R. Geoffrey Broderick, and I have been a veterinary surgeon for over forty-seven years. My life has been dedicated to making animals healthier and helping them to live longer. I'm not a marketer or advertising executive. I've never been part of a corporate product development team that uses reams of consumer data to create a product that satisfies some "niche" in the market.

Instead, I am a scientist, a passionate advocate for animals, and a practicing nutritionist and veterinarian. I have a busy clinic in the Southdown section of Huntington, Long Island, New York, where I treat animals with the same philosophy that progressive physicians of human naturopathic and alternative medicine are now using to treat people. I've seen incredible things in the course of my daily work: I have seen sick animals healed and animals with "allergies" regain their vigor, regrow their coats, and regain their youthful vitality. I have seen tumors shrink and disappear, and animals debilitated and dying from diabetes become "reborn" without the need for insulin.

Most important, I have learned to help animals help themselves to build their immune systems through real, organic nutrition so they won't get sick in the first place. The animals under my care live longer, happier, and healthier lives—all through the power of real food.

I practice health care and prevention and teach it to my clients. I practice *health care*—not sick care.

Just as some doctors of human medicine are recognizing the power of nutrients and healing foods, I've proven through my own experience that the way we've been caring for our animals is all wrong. We should be focusing on preventing disease in the first place instead of treating it. We should focus on *health care* instead of "sick care." My work with nutrition has proven that many "sick" animals aren't really sick as much as they are deficient in vital nutrients. THEY ARE eating food containing ingredients that are making them sick. Looking back now, it seems like most of my life has led up to you holding this book in your hands.

I was born October 23, 1941, fifteen minutes before Libra turned to Scorpio, so my life, personality, and attitude was never confined within the boundaries of any single box or astrological sign. I've known since I was three years old that I loved animals and wanted to be an animal doctor so I could heal and protect them. My first pet was a cat named Pussywillow, and my childhood was home to cats, dogs, horses, and homing pigeons. By age ten, I was already accomplished in the study of breeding and genetics, mainly because of my work and experience with breeding competition homing pigeons.

I grew up in Queens, New York. The house I lived in was moved (while my mother and I were actually in the house) to make way for the Van Wyck Expressway, which is today the main route to JFK Airport. My mother was an English teacher in an underprivileged urban school, and my father was a famous fire captain with the New York City Fire Department (FDNY). In the eighth grade, I was accepted into the Newtown Annex High School. This was a prestigious high school for inner city kids who wanted to be farmers, ranchers, and veterinarians.

My days at Newtown, however, were cut short. At age thirteen, my family moved out of New York City to the town of Massapequa on Long Island. It would have been a three-hour round trip commute by train and bus from our new home back to Newtown in Queens, and out of concern for me, my father would not allow it. Therefore, I was forced to enroll in Massapequa High School. My dreams were shattered, and I only lasted about three weeks at my new school. Pretty soon, I was skipping school every day and hitchhiking ten miles to the Meadowbrook Polo Club in Bethpage, New York, where my true passion lived: my horse Brandy.

I didn't see any point to high school—they were trying to stuff algebra and novels into my brain. I was not interested in made-up stories about fictitious characters when all I really cared about was riding and dreaming about being a cowboy and rancher and taking care of animals.

The chronic truancy continued until early on the morning of my sixteenth birthday when I left a note asking my father to officially drop me out of high school. By the time he had awakened, I had already jumped on a Greyhound bus for South Florida, to join the Black Diamond Wild West Show and and become a rodeo cowboy.

In the Wild West Show, I rode bareback broncs and bulls at the county and state fairs in the eastern United States and Canada. We would come into a town and rodeo. When that fair was over, we would pack up our equipment, load the horses and cattle into huge livestock trailers, and drive to our next performance. We often ate by campfires and listened to the older Native American cowboys tell us how to treat injured or sick people and animals in a natural, herbal manner, and how to prevent sickness in the first place. This was their medicine—passed down through generations from the "grandfathers" to the modern medicine men and women who served as the doctors of their various tribes. When we were sick or injured, there was no time or money to go to a traditional Western doctor or hospital. We were constantly on the road, so *they* treated us and made us well.

We bathed and washed our clothes in rivers and streams. We chanted Native American songs by campfire at night and slept under the stars using our saddles as pillows. Our horses would nuzzle us awake in the morning to a new and adventurous day. It was a magical way to grow up.

At age seventeen I sought a new adventure so I enlisted in the U.S. Army, 82$^{ND}$ Airborne Division, where I became a paratrooper! I competed as a member of the Fort Bragg Rodeo Association in Fayetteville, North Carolina, and passed my jump school with flying colors. They referred to me as "Yankee Boy." I also studied nutrition and became a cook. In 1960, the U.S. Army sent me to Korea, where

I spent a year cooking healthy food for the troops and jumping from airplanes (when I wasn't flying one). While stationed in Korea, I spent time in both China and Japan studying how they prepared their traditional, healthy foods. The whole time, I still dreamed of becoming an animal doctor, but for a high school no-show it seemed like an impossible dream.

My fortune began to change after I got home from Korea at the age of nineteen. Within forty-eight hours of being back in the States, I drove down to Miami, Florida, and enrolled in the famous Embry-Riddle Aeronautical Institute—not only to get my commercial pilot's license but also to study aeronautical engineering. This was one of the world's premier flight schools; it was started by members of the Flying Tigers, where they trained officers and pilots, some of whom went on to become famous test pilots and even astronauts.

Instead of going to high school, I had been flying aircraft since I was fifteen years old both Stateside and in Korea. At first I didn't believe it when they accepted me. "You guys don't know who I am!" I said. After all, being a high school truant with no high school credits—how could they let me attend a college in aeronautical engineering for pilots? Fortunately for me, the instructors at Embry-Riddle saw potential. They let me come to their flying school and enrolled me in a highly concentrated prep school program. This time around, I loved school—flying and skydiving on the weekends and going to rigorous mathematical and navigation classes during the week. It was heaven—but it still wasn't clear how I'd attain my dream of working with animals.

On Thanksgiving break in 1961, Farmingdale State College in New York (now the State University of New York at Farmingdale) was holding the New York state college entrance exams. This was the same college where I'd earned the highest score in a beef cattle management adult night school course at age fifteen. My dad encouraged me to go down and take the test.

Back in Miami, about five days later, a call came in from the State Education Department in Albany, the state capitol of New York, inviting me to attend any college or university of my choice in the state of New York. I said, "Wait a minute, doctor, how did you get my tests results back so fast?"

He replied, "Because your score was unlike that of anyone else who took the test!"

I picked SUNY Delhi. There I joined the first class of veterinary technicians ever taught in the United States and worked toward my associate degree.

It had been an incredible journey from the pristine polo grounds of Meadowbrook to the rodeo circuit, then to war-torn Korea, followed by flight school in Miami, and now to dreamy Delhi College nestled in the beautiful Catskill Mountains—but it wasn't over yet. While still at Delhi, I got a call from Dean Louis at Kansas State University, asking me to transfer to his college. I'll never forget what he told me: "There are a few moments in a lifetime that are defining. This is one of them. Come to Kansas State and prove yourself and you will get into my veterinary medical school."

Switching to Kansas State University and graduating with my baccalaureate, I became the first person to receive a degree from Kansas State without going to high school since the founding of this college in 1863. Suddenly, a path had opened up for me to obtain my impossible dream, and I was accepted into the hallowed halls of Kansas State University's revered College of Veterinary Medicine.

Every day in vet school was a learning adventure, and it was there that my comprehensive approach toward animal nutrition really took root. In my senior year, I took the first course in veterinary nutrition ever offered at any veterinary college in the United States. This one course changed my way of thinking. In that class, I realized there was a much better method to feed and raise healthy animals. In some ways, it was a revolutionary approach, but in many ways it went back to the old days before we figured out how to mass-produce animal food. This class would form the basis of my life's work.

While attending Kansas State, I married "the girl across the street" from New York. Yvonne joined me in Kansas and worked as the head nurse on the obstetrics floor at Saint Mary's Hospital at Kansas State. She delivered thirty-eight babies on her own while the doctors were out on farm calls. My son, Geoffrey, was born at

Saint Mary's. Today, we have been married for fifty-two years and have : three children and two grandchildren, Ava Yvonne and Peyton.

Graduation day was a monumental day for me. When I finally graduated with my Doctorate of Veterinary Medicine (DVM) in 1969 from Kansas State University, college officials told me I was the first doctor they knew of in the history of the United States to graduate with any kind of advanced medical or doctorate degree—human or veterinary—without a high school education. Believe me, this was no accident. When I say that my purpose in life is to improve animal nutrition—to make your pets healthier and live longer—this is why every step of my life, everything that has happened to me to bring me to this point, seemed like a small piece of a large, predetermined puzzle that led to my unique experience and perspective on animal nutrition.

After graduation, I quickly founded my own veterinary practice. From the beginning, I wanted to create a different kind of practice—one that brought the same principles of preventive medicine to animals that a handful of progressive physicians were applying to their human patients.

This was a novel concept at the time and I want to give credit to my mentor at Kansas State University, the great Dr. Russell Frey. It was Dr. Frey who authored the first course in veterinary nutrition and who sparked my interest in food as medicine for animals. He became my mentor, and I became his protégé and life-long friend. Before Dr. Frey, few people had thought much about pet food—in fact, the whole idea of commercial pet food was still fairly new. Mass-produced pet food was still making inroads throughout the country, and America's pets were worse off for it.

What I wanted to do was take pet food back to the old days, when pets were regularly fed table scraps in addition to what they acquired by hunting in barns and fields. Back in those days, it wasn't uncommon to see dogs and cats living more than twice as long than the eight or nine years we think of as normal today.

The key was to unlock the secrets of great pet nutrition. I started by seeking out the highest-quality pet food I could find for the animals that came into my office, which in those days was produced by one of the largest pet food companies in the business. I believed so strongly in the power of food that I quickly became the nation's leading veterinarian in the distribution of their veterinary diet products. I was even offered the presidency of the company. It was an amazing opportunity, but I turned it down when I found out that the company was about to be purchased by one of the largest growing food conglomerates. I couldn't be certain that we'd be allowed to continue producing top-quality pet food, and I was told that my plans to make massive improvements in this company's formulas had little or no chance of being adopted by the new owner.

That's when I realized that if I wanted the perfect pet food, I'd have to create it myself. So I went to work, cooking up the nation's first natural, organic pet food. It was called Cornucopia, and the original batches were created in my own house and office. My son Geoffrey and I caught bunker fish and canned the ground fish in Ball mason jars. Based on that early recipe, I experimented— adding different ingredients and seeing the results with my own eyes. Cornucopia wasn't your typical pet food. We didn't just rely on one protein. In addition to fish, we packed those cans with all different types of healthy, fresh animal proteins and healthy fats.

The results were amazing. I was seeing animals come into my office with allergies and autoimmune disorders that cleared up after a few months on my food. I watched older animals regain their mobility and youthful vitality. Obese animals slimmed down, and common diseases were rare among the pets under my care. The most common observation, which continues to this day, was from my clients worldwide, who told me, "My pets are growing younger!"

It wasn't long before my work in the area of pet nutrition was recognized. On March 18, 1978, at the fiftieth anniversary of the discovery of vitamin C held in Palm Springs, California, I received an award from the Committee for World Health. The award was for my research proving that vitamin C cured, corrected, controlled, and prevented cystitis (a urinary bladder inflammation/infection)—purported to be one of the leading diseases of both cats and women in America—by acidification of the urinary tract with use of oral ascorbic acid (vitamin C).

Almost two years to the day later, on March 15, 1980, I received an award from the Orthomolecular Medical Society at its convention in San Francisco, California, for my work and paper demonstrating, through time lapse radiography, the dissolving of a golf-ball size, triple-phosphate (struvite) stone (cystolith) by orthomolecular means. The term "orthomolecular" was coined by Linus Pauling to mean "the right molecules in the right amounts" (ortho is Greek for "right"). This was the first time in history a stone of this type had been dissolved instead of having to be surgically removed.

What was happening? Was it some kind of miracle?

Not at all. It was simply reality. The animals thrived because they were eating better food. This isn't so different from what has happened with people over the past decades. Today, the news is full of stories of "lifestyle diseases" that are killing millions of Americans: obesity, diabetes, metabolic syndrome, heart disease, chronic fatigue syndrome (CFS), and cancer. If you've even casually glanced at the health section in your local bookstore lately, you've no doubt seen the rows and rows of books touting the power of a healthy diet and lifestyle—all backed up by hundreds of high-quality clinical studies.

It's the same with our animals—maybe even more so. Now, decades into the age of mass-produced, low-quality pet food, we are reaping the bitter results. Record numbers of our companion animals are obese, and we have been conditioned to think it's normal to accept shortened lifespans, diabetes, heart and joint disorders, bone diseases, kidney failure, pancreatitis, and once-rare cancers killing increasing numbers of our animal children.

This isn't normal, and we don't have to accept it. Over my forty-seven years of feeding and treating companion animals, I've seen the amazing results a healthy diet can create. My program isn't radical, as much as it is a new paradigm for treating animals with healthy, real organic food. This paradigm represents a return to the way things were before big corporations figured out how to produce and successfully market billions of tons of low-quality "pet food" that fails to nourish and support the health and longevity of the animals we love.

My paradigm takes us back to the time of our grandparents who fed their pets what they ate from the table. This does not mean that your pets are sitting at the table or disturbing your dinner. It simply means that, after your dinner is completed, you empty your plates of healthy leftovers into your pet's dish instead of into your garbage can, which you were told to do by almost every healthcare professional that you ever encountered from the time you were a child.

This all came about because of a blatant, malicious lie that was perpetrated by the pet food cartel. The sole reason for this lie was to avoid your natural table food from competing with their beautifully packaged, brilliantly advertised, excessively promoted industrial waste products that have been mixed together and run through an extruder, puffed up and expanded into appetizing shapes and sizes, covered with sweeteners and grease, then labeled as "complete and balanced pet food" that you yourself would never dare to eat nor feed to your two-legged children.

I'm excited to share the results of my continuing life's work so that you too can see what real food can do for your pets.

# CHAPTER TWO

# Pet Nutrition: What You Need to Understand

Let's start at the beginning. In general, pet food has a few basic purposes:

**1. Food must meet the animal's energy needs.** Simply put, food provides energy that is essential for life. Food's primary job is to provide enough calories (a unit of energy measurement) so the body can maintain its normal function.

When it comes to pet food, energy is measured by the amount of *metabolizable energy*, or ME, in the bag or can. We'll explore this subject in greater depth later, but it's important to understand that ME is not a fixed value for any particular kind of food. Instead, the ME of a pet food depends on both what's in the food, such as the amount and proportion of the various ingredients and the quality of the ingredients, and the animal that's eating it. Because it can be very expensive to analyze ME through direct feeding trials with actual animals, the pet food industry often uses a mathematical formula to estimate or calculate the ME of different foods for different species. Today, all pet foods on the market are evaluated for ME calculated, and the results of those tests should be noted clearly and largely on the packaging.

It's my opinion that these requirements are the bare minimum—it's like thinking a person can live on fast food. Sure, it's possible to get through your day, but it's not optimal for health. ME from protein is more expensive and much more valuable than the same ME using cheap carbs. This is where ME fails as a true measure of the value of food and is misleading and advantageous to the producers of cheap carb-laden foods.

Let me explain. Carbohydrates yield 4 Kcal/gram. Protein yields the same 4 Kcal/gram. Fat yields 9 Kcal/gram, thus making fat the highest source of energy. Fat is an extremely necessary ingredient, as well as the most expensive ingredient. Protein is the second most expensive ingredient and is highly valuable nutritionally. Carbohydrates are the cheapest source of energy and the least valuable of any source of energy. Carbohydrates are the problem-causing elements in the nutritional chain.

The important thing to remember is that when you measure ME and you're using high-quality fat, which is expensive, and high-quality protein, which is expensive, you are producing an expensive but highly usable and highly nutritious diet. When you add carbs to the diet, you are adding a non-valuable, cheap entity for the purpose of making a less valuable food simply to keep the price down and the profits up. Therefore, you can have a product with a high ME by using cheap carbs instead of expensive protein because they both yield 4 Kcal/gram. The high-carb diet is far less valuable to the animal eating it, but the carb-laden product can be sold at a cheaper price that appears more attractive to the uneducated consumer.

The conclusion is that the ME shows you the level of the caloric density but *it does not distinguish between those calories that are nutritious and those calories that are empty*. Our quest here is to teach you to provide your pet with real, nutritious organic foods and to cease feeding your beloved pet inferior, high-carb junk food.

**2. *Food must provide essential nutrients.*** Essential nutrients are those that cannot be manufactured inside the body and have to be consumed in the diet. Animals without adequate essential nutrients will quickly begin to show symptoms of a nutrient deficiency. If this sounds similar to the requirements of humans, it is only because humans are animals as well.

The organization that determines the basic nutritional profile of pet food is called the Association of American Feed Control Officials, or AAFCO. This group doesn't have any actual statutory powers, meaning it can't enforce pet food quality laws, but the group's standards have been adopted by most of the states. We'll get more into this later, but for now it's enough to know that when you're looking at a pet food label, it's probably using AAFCO's formulas and methods to determine the nutritional content of the food.

Unfortunately, this doesn't tell us that the food is actually nutritious. The biggest problem in most cases is that the food doesn't pack in enough of the important macronutrients in the optimal proportions. This leads to pet food that is technically "filling" but also full of *empty calories*, which in turn can cause several rampant problems among pets: hunger, overfeeding, obesity, and all the horrible diseases that go along with it.

## MACRONUTRIENTS, MICRONUTRIENTS, AND YOUR PET'S FOOD

Animal nutrition and human nutrition are very similar. Just like humans, pets need adequate amounts of macronutrients to stay vibrant and healthy. Macronutrients are the foundation of a good diet—they are the foods that animals need in relatively large quantities to maintain health. The three macronutrients are: carbohydrates, fats, and proteins.

## CARBOHYDRATES

The easiest way to think about carbohydrates is to regard them as sugars, starch, and fiber. Carbohydrates provide the body with a quick source of energy (4 Kcal/gram of ME). Carbohydrates are typically derived from plants, such as potatoes, turnips and other root vegetables, and grains like corn, wheat, barley, rye, soy, rice, sorghum, and any other grains. Once they're ingested, carbohydrates are broken down in the intestines and metabolized into a special kind of sugar called glucose. When carbohydrates reach the digestive tract, they initiate a signal from the digestive tract to the pancreas to secrete insulin into the bloodstream. When the glucose reaches the bloodstream, the insulin is waiting to force the glucose into the body's fat cells and lock it away in those cells, reducing glucose in the bloodstream.

Glucose is the body's main form of energy. When the glucose is taken out of the bloodstream by the action of insulin, the energy level of you and your animal drops. Your need for more energy makes you feel hungry again. This is why, shortly after eating carbs, you feel hungry again and so does your pet. So what do all of you animals do? You look for, and find, more food. The main thing you need to know about carbohydrates is that excess carbohydrates are stored by the body as fat, so a diet heavy in carbohydrates will lead to recurring hunger, snacking, eating, and obesity in you and your pets. In other words, carbs will *make your animal fat* just like carbs make you fat.

A second type of carbohydrate is known as fiber. In dogs and cats, fiber plays a much different role than it does in herbivores like horses and cows, which can actually break down most types of fiber to use as energy. Because carnivores like dogs and cats have shorter digestive tracts, they cannot break down many types of fiber. The correct form, fermentable fiber, generally improves the digestive process, cleans the gut, and slows down the absorption of sugar, which is very important for dogs and cats, as well as people. The faster one absorbs sugar the more toxic it is.

## FATS

Fats are frequently misunderstood. Many people assume that fatty foods are bad for their animals because "fat will make my animal fat." In fact, dogs and (especially) cats need relatively high quantities of fats. The key is to provide the right *kinds* of fats. Broadly speaking, fats can be classified as saturated, monounsaturated, and polyunsaturated fats. The science behind dietary fat can be complicated, but the main point you need to understand as a pet owner is that the right fats are an essential and healthy part of your pet's diet. *Fats do NOT make your animal fat.*

Fats serve a number of critical roles in the canine or feline body, including:

- Insulation. The layer of fat directly under the skin, called subcutaneous fat, provides protection from the elements.
- Energy storage. Animals are very efficient at storing energy as fat, which is the most energy-dense macronutrient and provides the most energy per pound of any food type. Fat yields 9 Kcal/gram.
- Proper nerve and brain function. Nerve and brain cells are made up of fatty acids, especially omega-3 fatty acids.
- Making food taste good!

In recent years, there has been an explosion of research into the health benefits of a special class of essential fatty acids (EFAs) in the omega-3 and omega-6 families. Omega-6 fatty acids include linoleic acid, which is derived from certain vegetable oils as well as poultry and pork fat. Omega-3 fatty acids include alpha-linolenic acid (ALA), which can be converted into EPA (eicosapentaenoic acid) and DHA (docosahexaenoic acid). These omega-3 fatty acids can be found at high levels in certain fish, especially cold-water fish like salmon and tuna. They are the *anti-freeze* of the fish in the sense that they help keep the fish's blood flowing, even in very cold temperatures. Omega-3s in plant form are also found in fresh-ground flax seed, chlorella, spirulina, and blue-green algae.

The array of health benefits attributed to the EFAs is astonishing. Most of the research into these powerful healthy fats has been done in humans, where they have been shown to reduce the risk of heart disease and cancer, aid in brain function, keep the eyes healthy, and even prevent obesity. What little research has been done in animals on EFAs has supported these benefits for them too and has shown that adequate EFAs can help your pet's coat and skin stay healthy.

The most important thing to understand about EFAs is that the balance between omega-6 and omega-3 fatty acids is critical. Diets that are too high in omega-6 fatty acids—which include those based on grains—can actually be harmful and lead to increased disease and inflammation. The best pet foods provide not only adequate amounts of dietary fat, but also the right proportion of saturated and unsaturated fats and the correct ratio between omega-6 and omega-3 fatty acids. Ideally, I recommend that you provide fat from animal sources instead of plant-based sources like grains, and oils from grains, such as: corn (germ) oil, wheat (germ) oil, cottonseed oil, rapeseed oil (the GMO oil known as canola oil), etc.

# PROTEINS

Proteins are the final macronutrient. Proteins are made up of amino acids and have multiple critical functions, including:

- Providing structure for organs and connective tissue
- Building muscle
- Forming the building blocks of enzymes that regulate metabolic activity
- Forming the building block of hormones
- Transporting oxygen and nutrients
- Providing 4 Kcal/gram of ME

Because proteins are made from amino acids, it's essential to have adequate levels of amino acids. In all, there are twenty-two amino acids. Of these twenty-two, dogs can only make twelve internally. Because these amino acids are made internally, they are known as *nonessential amino acids*. The remaining ten amino acids must be provided through the diet of dogs. These ten amino acids are known as *essential amino acids* because it is essential that they come from the diet.

Cats, on the other hand, have a critical need for another amino acid they cannot internally manufacture like the dog does. This extra essential amino acid is called taurine. The cat requires *eleven amino acids* in its diet out of the twenty-two amino acids in total.

In general, the best way to guarantee adequate levels of the various amino acids is to *provide varied and adequate protein* sources. It's a little bit of a loop, but dietary protein can be broken down into amino acids, which are then used to create new proteins in the body. One of the many benefits that a dog gets from eating a food that is designed for cats is extra taurine.

Fortunately, getting your dog or cat to eat adequate protein isn't very difficult. Protein is naturally present in all meat products, including seafood, and as we all know, cats and dogs love meat! However, there is a key difference between a merely adequate diet and a superior diet. As you can probably guess, not all proteins are the same. In fact, different proteins have different levels of the various amino acids, and they aren't equally digestible (meaning that some proteins are harder to digest and harder to metabolize than others).

There are a number of measures pet food scientists use to measure the ultimate value of a protein, but the important thing to understand is that a truly healthy diet provides a *wealth of different types of protein.*

The best of all the proteins is the one with the highest *biological value* or usability by the body. This perfect protein is found in eggs. Whole eggs have always been an essential part of the real foods I have formulated and developed throughout my career as a veterinary nutritionist. You should *always* mix in your leftover plain eggs with your real food for pets.

If you think of a healthy diet like a house, then the three *macronutrients* are the foundation and structure. The *micronutrients* are everything else. Micronutrients include the vitamins and minerals that are essential for life. They are called micronutrients because only very small amounts are needed for optimal health. This doesn't mean, however, that they aren't important—deficiencies in vitamins and minerals can be deadly.

Once again, AAFCO has established guidelines for the minimum level of vitamins and minerals in pet food in the AAFCO Dog Food Nutrient Profile and the AAFCO Cat Food Nutrient Profile. Most states have adopted these standards, so consumers can rest assured that whatever pet food they're buying, even the cheapest generic pet food, adheres to a certain minimum standard in its nutrient profile.

It's important to remember, however, that these AAFCO standards represent the minimum your pet will need. AAFCO standards were never meant to be used as an "ideal" standard for pet nutrition. Instead, just like the USDA human standards, they represent an excellent starting point for basic pet nutrition, not the final word. So there is nothing wrong with AAFCO standards. There is, however, something wrong with companies that market cheap food that meets only the barest threshold as a "complete" food option for your pet.

In fact, in my opinion, feeding your animal a cheap food that contains only the minimum will not sustain your pet through a long and healthy, disease-free life. Just like you might take a multivitamin every morning, most pets will benefit from going above and beyond these minimums. *That's what this book is all about.*

I believe, through simple common sense, that a healthy person who does not get sick will live longer than a person who is frequently sick.

Table 1.1 lists the major vitamins and minerals measured by AAFCO alongside symptoms of deficiencies and dietary sources.

| SYMPTOMS OF DEFICIENCY: VITAMINS | | |
|---|---|---|
| Vitamin A (fat soluble) | Reduced growth and impaired reproductive capabilities; skin problems | Fish, dairy, liver, egg yolks |
| Vitamin D (fat soluble) | Bone disease, hormone imbalance | Liver, fish, egg yolk, exposure to sun |
| Vitamin E (fat soluble) | Reproductive disorders, feline pansteatitis (an inflammatory disorder) | Wheat, soybean and corn oils |

## SYMPTOMS OF DEFICIENCY: VITAMINS

| | | |
|---|---|---|
| Vitamin K (fat soluble) | Blood clotting disorders and increased risk of hemorrhage | Green leafy plants, liver, fish |
| Thiamin (water soluble B vitamin) | Central nervous system disorders, weight loss | Meat, wheat germ brewers yeast, nutritional yeast |
| Riboflavin (water soluble B vitamin) | Central nervous system disorders, skin problems | Dairy, organ meats, many vegetables |
| Niacin (water soluble B vitamin) | Black tongue disease | Meat, grains |
| Pyridoxine (water soluble B vitamin) | Anemia | Organ meat, wheat germ, fish |
| Pantothenic acid (water soluble B vitamin) | Anorexia | Liver, kidney, legumes, dairy |
| Biotin (water soluble B vitamin) | Skin problems | Eggs, milk, liver, legumes |

| SYMPTOMS OF DEFICIENCY: VITAMINS | | |
|---|---|---|
| Folic acid (water soluble B vitamin) | Anemia, low white blood cell count | Organ meats, green leafy vegetables |
| Cobalamin (water soluble B vitamin) | Anemia | Meat, fish, poultry |
| Choline (water soluble B vitamin) | Neurological disorders, liver disease | Egg yolks, organ meats, legumes, dairy products |
| Vitamin C (water soluble) | Not essential for dogs or cats | Adrenal Glands |
| *Source: Canine and Feline Nutrition, 3RD Ed.* | | |

| SYMPTOMS OF DEFICIENCY: MINERALS | | |
|---|---|---|
| Calcium | Weak bones, hormone imbalance | Dairy, poultry and meat meal, bone |
| Phosphorus | Weak bones, hormone imbalance | Meat, fish, poultry |
| Magnesium | Soft tissue disorders, muscular problems | Soybean, corn, bone meal |

| SYMPTOMS OF DEFICIENCY: MINERALS | | |
|---|---|---|
| Sulfur | None known | Meat, fish, poultry |
| Iron | Anemia | Organ meats |
| Copper | Anemia, impaired bone growth | Organ meats |
| Zinc | Skin and coat disorders, slow growth, repro-ductive disorders | Beef liver, poultry dark meat, milk, egg yolk, legumes |
| Manganese | Reproductive disorders, slow growth | Meat, poultry, fish |
| Iodine | Goiter, slow growth, repro-ductive disorders | Fish, liver, beef |
| Selenium | Heart problems skeletal problems | Grains, meat, poultry |
| Cobalt | Anemia, vitamin B deficiency | Fish, dairy |
| *Source: Canine and Feline Nutrition, 3RD Ed.* | | |

In addition to these vitamins and minerals, dogs and cats also need a few trace elements, including: molybdenum, nickel, silicon, zinc, and vanadium. There is no established minimum guideline for these, but there is little doubt they are required for optimal health.

It's not especially important that pet owners understand the detailed biological function of each vitamin and mineral, but if you quickly scan down the right column of Table 1.1, you'll notice something very important: it would take a huge variety of foods—from meat and dairy products to a wide assortment of plant-based foods—to deliver all the needed vitamins and minerals.

This brings up an important point. Many vets and animal experts recommend finding a food your animal likes and then sticking with it, sometimes for life. While it's true that animals do have preferences in their food choices (just like we do!), it would be very hard for a single food to provide everything your animal needs for years and years.

This makes even more sense if you think about the way dogs and cats evolved in nature. In the natural world, cats and especially dogs eat a varied diet depending on what's available. While cats are more carnivorous than dogs and have some specialized dietary needs, wild cats still eat a variety of prey, and they'll eat all parts of the animal. Dogs, too, have evolved to eat a varied diet. Given their choice, wild dogs eat prey when they can catch it, beginning with the organ meats but also eating skin, bones, marrow, and muscle, and then they might snack on some grass, perhaps some berries, and maybe gnaw on a branch or nip at leaves and bark.

If you carry this forward, it's clear that feeding your pet the same food day after day, year after year, poses a challenge when it comes to supplying your animal with the complete range of nutrients they need to thrive. This is true even for AAFCO-approved pet foods, which are only formulated to provide the minimum levels of macronutrients and micronutrients. A pet that is merely existing is not necessarily a pet that is thriving and vibrantly healthy. By providing a more varied diet with a wide assortment of proteins, fats, and plant-based foods, you'll be giving your pet the gift of a longer, healthier life.

Although plant-based foods are not necessary for cats and can even be harmful because cats are not designed to eat, digest, or metabolize them, your outdoor cat will decide for itself what it will indeed consume for variety.

## WATER: AN ESSENTIAL ELEMENT

The last major element of animal nutrition is also one of the simplest: water. Both cats and dogs need access to clean, filtered drinking water at all times. Your pet's water requirement will fluctuate greatly, depending on how much exercise the animal gets, if they are pregnant or nursing, their size, the weather, how often they urinate (cats have the ability to concentrate their urine more than dogs, which reduces their water needs in times of low water supply), and how much water is in their food.

Instead of trying to figure out how much water your animal needs, it's much easier to simply keep their water bowl full of clean, filtered water—and filtering is important. You should never give your dog or cat tap water without filtering it at home.

One last word about water: we'll talk about this in greater depth in the next chapter, but pet food itself is also a source of water. For consistency's sake, pet food nutrition analysis is often expressed as a percentage of dry matter weight, but that doesn't change the fact that all pet foods contain at least some water. Obviously, dry foods have much less water in them than wet foods, so don't be surprised if your dog or cat that lives on wet food drinks less than an animal that lives on dry kibble. However, pet food should never be treated as a substitute for access to clean, fresh, filtered water. Don't give your pet water that you and your children wouldn't drink.

The unfortunate truth is that many canned, or "wet," pet food formulations are up to 90 percent water (or broth) and grain, so they have much less of the nutrient-dense fats and proteins your animal needs. It's much better to spend a little extra money on high-quality canned pet food containing high levels of healthy fats and proteins with less water (moisture) than it is to buy cheaper, water-logged grains that only supply the bare minimum of nutrients. This forces the animals to eat two or three times as much food to get their required nutrients. In the long run, there is no savings with "cheap" food.

## BONES

And let's not forget about bones! Cats and dogs have been eating bones for over twenty-nine million years. They teethe on bones as puppies and kittens. They get their minerals from bones. They clean their teeth on bones— not chemical toothpaste and chemical whiteners. They make milk from the minerals in bones. They get all the blessings of marrow from bones. It's a great idea to feed your pets fresh, raw, marrow bones.

There is a belief that cooked bones can shatter as they are chewed up and cause internal injuries. I have not experienced that problem. In fact, when you make bone broth out of chicken or turkey or salmon, you will find that the bones yield a soft, yet crunchy texture similar to the delicate and interesting mouth-feel of eating Scottish shortbread.

When feeding fresh, raw bones to your pets, I wouldn't worry about bacteria, since in the wild most bones get buried deeply in dirt, then are dug up and eaten at a later date. In my forty-seven plus years in veterinary medical practice, I have never seen a dog or cat die of "bone-itis." I have instead seen hundreds of animals die as a result of rotten, infected, tarter/plaque/calculi-ridden teeth and tooth loss, with critically inflamed and infected gums, because the animal was not allowed to chew on bones. Why? Because someone with a white jacket and a stethoscope around their neck was taught (with intimidation) by the manufacturer's sales "reps" to pass on (with intimidation) a fairy tale to the pet's parents that feeding bones was going to kill their pets. Why? So that they (the pet's parents) would buy fattening sugar "cookies" that were designed by some Madison Avenue illustrator to give the impression of a "bone" (that has no anatomical resemblance to any bone in the body) that crumbled when the pet bit down on it, leaving the pieces stuck between the dog's teeth but hardly cleaned anything. OK! The same lie goes for dry pet food.

## AND SPEAKING OF FAIRY TALES, "WHERE'S THE 'MILK'?"

Here is an amazing story: It was an early spring forty-seven years ago when we, the Class of '69, were called into the lecture room to hear a seminar presented by the major manufacturer of dog biscuits. Two big "suits" came strolling in and the intimidation began. These expert sales reps informed us that feeding bones to our pets was highly detrimental to their health and welfare. The reason being that the bones will get stuck in their throat, esophagus, stomach, and intestinal tract. Even worse, they could perforate any of these organs. In either case, surgery would be necessary and we would be responsible as doctors because we failed to warn the clients "never to feed a bone."

The penalty for this malpractice and incompetence (and disobeying the indoctrination of the pet food cartel) was that the veterinarian would be at least obliged to repair the pet at his/her own expense and also face the liability of a lawsuit for not practicing this fictitious "standard of care." The suits knew then and still know today that most medical students were—and are—young, inexperienced, impressionable, programmable, and subordinate. These reps did—and still do—their jobs well because they know that upon graduation, these children will suddenly become *doctors* and it will be their turn to do the "programming" to the people their egos will consider their subordinates.

So how will you know the difference between good food and cheap food? In the next chapter, we'll talk about how pet food is made and how to read a label to recognize high quality versus junk pet food.

# CHAPTER THREE

## How Is Pet Food Made Anyway?

I T'S NOT UNCOMMON FOR PET OWNERS TO BE confused and even worried about the food they feed their pets. In most of our homes, the family pet (or pets!) is a full member of the household. The days of taking our companion animals for granted or viewing them as work animals have long since passed. Most cats aren't mousing in their homes, and few dogs are working dogs. Today, pet owners bring their furry companions into their lives just because they love their animals, and the animals provide them with unconditional love.

Yet even as our historical relationship to our pets has changed, it's become more confusing than ever to figure out how we can provide the healthiest lifestyle for our animals. In this chapter, we're going to discuss how people fed their pets historically, how that changed with the industrialization of pet food, and what you can do today to give your pet the very best.

When you realize that dogs and cats have been domesticated for thousands of years, it's easier to understand how the idea of "pet food" is a relatively new concept. For most of their time with people, dogs and cats have been considered work animals. Cats were generally allowed to run wild and were expected to hunt for their food. Whether it was keeping ships, barns, or cathedrals free from vermin, it was a rare cat that got more than an occasional saucer of milk from its human "owners."

The plight of dogs wasn't much different—although it may have been even more focused on work. Dogs have always seemed like the perfect companions for a good reason: when it comes to working with people, they are by far the most eager animals on earth. Historically, they were trained to do many of the same things people expect from their dogs today: shepherding, hunting, guarding, and even hauling loads.

Throughout all of these many centuries of living together, companion animals were usually fed table scraps. Naturally, as the human diet improved, our animals' diets improved also. By the 18$^{TH}$ and 19$^{TH}$ centuries, many animals were thriving on a steady diet of table scraps and homemade human food.

Think about the life of a farm cat, for example. The cat enjoyed some fresh, whole milk in the morning after the milking was done, followed by a meal of a fresh rodent, and then after dinner was over, some delicious table scraps if they were interested. The same went for dogs—they enjoyed a diet of fresh milk and a wonderfully varied selection of table scraps that might include everything from grains and breads to cooked vegetables and fresh fruit to fresh meat. The meat was always fresh because, generally, there was no refrigeration.

Note that milk came fresh from the cow. There was no pasteurization that destroyed enzymes and nutrients in the milk. There was no homogenization that destroyed the fat composition, and it was not skimmed to remove the precious fat (cream), which is the most expensive part of the milk. There was no dilution of the natural milk. There was no genetically modified (GMO) addition of recombinant bovine growth hormone (rBGH) that made cows develop mastitis in the attempt to force increased milk production.

Even though very few (if any) animals had access to the same kinds of advanced veterinary care that's available today, it wasn't uncommon to see animals living twice as long as we expect our animals to live today. Even in our grandparents' days, dogs could live to be twenty years old—or older—as they typically do to this day in rural Latin American countries. Cats could live far, far past the age of twenty. In fact, this is still true in many places of the world. In Third World countries, where it's easy to assume that animals receive substandard veterinary care, a steady diet of varied table scraps has the same effect: it's common to find very old dogs and cats in places that might surprise you.

Why would animals fed on table scraps live so long and fare so well? Because they ate a healthy, varied diet of high-quality food—and food is the best kind of medicine.

In the United States, this pattern began to change, slowly at first, with the introduction of commercial pet food. The very first known "dog food" (meaning it was sold specifically for dogs) was introduced in 1860 by a man named James Spratt. Spratt was an "ex-pat" American living in London, when he introduced the first dog biscuit. It sold well enough that he soon launched an American version.

In 1908, the original Milk-Bone was introduced and named the "Maltoid" dog biscuit. Not long after, in 1922, Ken-L-Ration introduced the very first canned dog food. In 1956, dry dog food came out in the form of large sacks that were sold in farm and feed stores. These sacks made feeding pets more convenient and easier than ever before. The dry-baked sheets of dog food were broken into pieces called "kibbles."

When the U.S. entered World War II in 1941, canned pet food ruled the tiny market. At the time, about 90 percent of the small amount of commercial pet food sold in the United States was canned food (which was hard to get because the metal for the cans was used for the war effort). This canned food was different than the canned food we see today—it was made exclusively from by-products of human food, then cooked and canned with little thought to formulation or nutritional content. In fact, much of it was horsemeat. By the end of World War II in September 1945, the average urban market carried a few brands of bagged dry dog food and still more cans of wet dog food.

In the 1950s, a new technology entered the market and changed everything. During the period of rapid industrialization that followed the end of the Korean War in July of 1953, a company called Purina figured out how to create what became known as "expanded" pet food. This was right around the same time that TV dinners and hydrogenated and liquid vegetable oils were introduced for people. None of these developments were any better for animals than they were for us.

The new expanded pet foods were created by mixing and grinding various ingredients together, then flash-cooking the mixture and forcing it through a steam pressure cooker. This process was called extrusion. Extrusion caused the food particles to expand rapidly, giving it a lighter texture and better taste than the previous dry biscuits. For good measure, the resulting extruded pellets, called "kibble," were sprayed with a coating of fat or some other flavor enhancer.

The first of these expanded dog foods, Purina Dog Chow, was introduced in 1956 and quickly became the top-selling dog food in the country. Within a year, the pet food market was a $350 million market (and that's in late 1950's dollars). Today, expanded pet foods still make up the majority of the pet food market, which, according to the APPA (American Pet Products Association) statistics for 2015, is estimated at $23.04 billion dollars in the United States alone. This is a billion dollars more than 2014.

Not only is the pet food market growing, but so is the number of pet-owning households. In 1988, 56 percent of US households owned a pet. In the 2015–2016 American Pet Products Association (APPA) National Pet Owner's Survey, 65 percent of US households owned a pet, which equates to 79.7 million homes with pets.

In the 1970s, a handful of pioneering veterinary doctors and animal nutritionists, including me, began to think of better ways to feed companion animals—but we were far ahead of the curve. AAFCO was founded in the early twentieth century, but it wasn't until 1990 that the group introduced its nutrition profiles for dogs and cats. Before that, the National Research Council, which worked under the auspices of the National Academy of Sciences, put out annual research reports on pet nutrition, even though these requirements carried little weight in the real world.

Instead of focusing on animal nutrition, their focus was on cost and contamination—but mostly for human foods. Pet foods were widely considered a good way to use up the by-products and not-fit-for-human-consumption waste that came out of the fat rendering business from slaughterhouses and agricultural processing facilities. These waste products included bakery and candy waste, plus the waste of liquor and alcohol distillery factories. In fact, when commercial pet foods were first introduced, the main concern among shoppers was that these foods shouldn't be sold alongside human food—there was the concern that adulterated pet food would somehow "contaminate" human food.

This is the environment in which the movement toward healthier, natural, pet food was created. In those days, in the early 1970s, anybody producing higher-quality pet food was likely making small batches in their garage or a small kitchen. There really wasn't a market for higher-quality, healthier pet foods.

Fortunately for the animals, this changed, along with the growing awareness of the problems with our human diet. Just as people slowly woke up to the problems associated with a diet heavy in processed foods, salt, carbs, and sugar, enlightened pet owners began to realize that their pets would also benefit from a return to basics. Pet foods like my own Cornucopia, were designed to provide optimal nutrition—and it's fortunate that plenty of pet owners were ready to hear my message.

I remember sitting with Gloria Swanson and her husband William Dufty at the Health and Nutrition Expo in New York City in the 1970s. Bill had written the story of Billy Holiday called Lady Sings the Blues and now he was introducing his new book, Sugar Blues, a masterpiece calling attention to the detrimental effects of sugar on our lives. When he finished his lecture, Bill called me to the podium, where I declared a national war against sugar and chemicals in pet foods. Before then, few people—if any—had publicly called for improved standards in pet food, and the idea of natural, organic food was ridiculed as extravagant. This was the commencement of the natural pet food movement and industry in America.

It was rough taking on the established pet food cartel, but it was my calling. We needed to eliminate BHT, BHA, ethoxyquin, propylene glycol, artificial flavors, artificial colors, monosodium glutamate (MSG), and sugar in pet food for the same reason that many natural health enthusiasts wanted to remove them from human food: they had no nutritional value, and in some cases, contributed to sickness and diseases, sometimes leading to death.

Fortunately, I had a background in a different tradition. During my teenage rodeo years, I had learned natural preservation techniques from the nomadic Native American tribes of the Southwest. My adversaries in the pet food industry called us "Doctor Broderick and his Band of Indians." I remain truly grateful to my Native American teachers and friends, who were the unpublished, unselfish, spiritual, giving, aboriginal, indigenous occupants of this amazing American part of Mother Earth.

All these efforts paid off. Today, all you have to do is walk down any pet food aisle to see the strong focus on healthier foods. You'll see foods advertising all sorts of ingredients and nutrients, such as "Omega-3s for healthier coats," "Glucosamine and chondroitin for joint repair" or "A variety of game and fish." This is a very positive development for our animals, because it demonstrates that owners care, but it does present a new challenge: sifting through the marketing claims to find the truly healthy foods. If you're savvy enough to be able to weed through the ridiculous advertising hype, it will become obvious that you are left with slim pickins.

Some people never "got it." By the 1980s, I was doing twenty-six pet-related trade shows and conferences a year. I was constantly running into members of competing pet food companies, who would yell to me, "Hey, Doc, lookie here! We have a 'natural' pet food too!" I would reply, "You have sugar in your stuff. Sugar is not natural for the animals!" They would laugh and rebut with, "Sugar is found in nature, Doc, so it qualifies as 'natural!'"

Sugar, aspartame, and MSG are allowed to be added into pet foods to get the animals hooked on it by making it sweet. It's all done under the guise of "natural flavors." These technicalities are how they are constantly hooking the animals, just like they have done to all of us. "If Mikey don't like it, sweeten it!"

It all begins with the label.

# CHAPTER FOUR

# How to Read a Pet Food Nutrition Label

IN MANY WAYS, READING A PET FOOD LABEL IS FAMILIAR territory for anyone who's ever read the nutrition panel on human food. The format is basically the same, including the listing of ingredients in order of declining weight, the breakdown of macronutrients including crude protein, crude fat, and crude fiber, and the listing of various nutrients contained within the food. That said, however, there are some crucial differences when it comes to pet food that every pet owner should be aware of.

The first is the use of guaranteed analysis measurements. According to the AAFCO measurements that most pet food labels use, ingredient panels have to list minimum and maximum amounts of nutrients in any particular product. Thus, a product might have a listing of "minimum crude fat: 12%." This means that a product cannot have less than the twelve percent listed on the label...but it can have more. Thus, one product listing 12 percent minimum fat might have the twelve percent on the label, while another might have 14 percent. Although it only seems like a small amount, this discrepancy can have a significant impact on the metabolic value of the food.

The most important thing to consider, however, is the overall water content of the food involved. It's a little bit complicated, but pet food labels are typically formulated on the "as fed" basis, instead of measuring them as a percentage of dry matter weight. This is true for both wet foods and dry foods. This means it can be virtually impossible to actually compare the nutrient density and value of different types of foods.

Wet foods, for example, might seem comparable to dry foods in terms of the overall nutrient profile—but that's only because the label doesn't account for the massive discrepancy between the two in terms of water content. The average dry dog food has a water content of about 10 or 12 percent; the average wet food has 80 percent or more water content. If you're curious how much water your pet food has, check out the label for water (moisture) content. It is required to be listed.

Simply looking at the crude fiber or crude protein content of any particular food and trying to compare it to a different type of food can be highly misleading. The foods might look the same on the label, but in reality, they pack a very different punch in terms of actual nutrients delivered to your pet. In fact, the only way to actually compare the nutrient values of different foods is to dry them to the same water content, then run sophisticated nutritional analysis of the foods along with expensive and difficult feeding tests. Obviously, this is beyond the reach of most pet owners.

So is there anything you can do to get an accurate idea of the quality of your pet food? Unfortunately, it only gets more complicated from here.

Many experts recommend using the ingredient list to determine the nutritional value of a pet food. While there are some important things you can learn from the ingredient list, this is far from a perfect measure. Looking at the ingredient list on a can of wet food, for example, you can get a general idea how much of the food is water. If you see water or broth listed as the first ingredient, for example, you're probably holding a can of food that is between 80 percent and 90 percent water. If broth and water are listed separately, then combined they will add up to the first ingredient.

The second ingredient might be listed as beef or chicken, making it easy to assume that while the food might have lots of water, it also has lots of rich, healthy proteins like beef or chicken. In many cases, however, this is highly deceptive. All this means is that the second ingredient is the second ingredient by weight, but it makes no guarantees about the composition of that particular ingredient. In other words, that ingredient could be mostly water too.

After that, pet food manufacturers are notorious for figuring out ways to hide less desirable ingredients. Take for example the common ingredients ground wheat, split wheat, and wheat flour. In fact, these are all different forms of the same ingredient: wheat. The same applies for brown rice, white rice, rice flour, and brewer's rice. Although these ingredients may appear relatively far down the ingredient list, when you add their weight together, you might end up with more overall weight for wheat or rice than any type of meat or protein.

When you break it down, this means that many of the most popular pet foods are actually composed of water, carbohydrates like rice and wheat—that soak up water and add bulk to the food—and meat protein that itself is mostly made up of water.

Amazingly, in many of these common pet foods, the main source of protein isn't the meat at all but rather textured vegetable protein, or TVP, which can appear far down the label. To make it even more confusing, this TVP is often shaped and colored to look like meat chunks, so that delicious "meat stew" you pour into your pet's bowl in reality is TVP chunks swimming in a stew of water and carbs.

And as you might also have guessed, just because a product lists an ingredient, it doesn't mean it's providing a high quality version of that ingredient. For example, a wet food that includes lamb or beef as its primary source would rarely list any information about the type of lamb or beef that's included, or what processing was done to the meat. As a result, you could be holding a super-premium food with calorically dense cuts of real beef next to a can of cheap food filled with water-soaked chunks of TVP, and never know the difference from the label. After all, both might list beef as the first or second ingredient. Without any way to accurately compare the foods, it can be easy to shop by price and end up giving your pet a far-less-than-optimal food. Even phosphates can be added to make fish, chicken, duck, lamb, and beef swell with water. Look carefully at the moisture content on the guaranteed analysis and where water or broth appears on the ingredient list.

With dry foods, it's not uncommon to see a protein like chicken, fish, or beef listed as the first ingredient. Beware! This can be highly misleading too. It might be true that one of these ingredients has the most water weight when it goes into the mouth of the extruder barrel. However, when it comes out the other end as a finished product, the chicken or other meat might have lost 80 percent of its mass through water evaporation. This means that if you put one hundred pounds of meat in one end and take the water out, you only have about twenty-two pounds of meat left as fat and protein after it comes out of the extruder and dryer. Technically, the water counts, because it is included in the uncooked ingredient.

On that same label, the second ingredient—dry meat meal—will actually often outweigh the chicken. Then come the peas and the rice and soy and fish meal. In reality, the chicken belongs in the fifth or sixth position, not the first, because it is now a dry ingredient just like the meals and other ingredients. Another highly misleading trick is to list peas, pea protein, pea fiber, and pea starch separately, because if they were listed together by weight as peas, they could become the first ingredient. Upon close observation of certain bags of pet foods, a person could realize they are simply buying a big bag of "pee."

Lastly, it's worth mentioning that many pet owners focus on the wrong ingredients on their pet food label. It's not uncommon for veterinary doctors to hear pet owners disparage foods with animal by-products in them, even as the same pet owners eagerly pay top dollar for wet foods that are 90 percent water by weight. But what are these by-products, exactly? Should you worry about them?

In truth, by-products are not great ingredients for your pets—but first you have to understand what a by-product actually is. In the wild, dogs and cats eagerly devour the liver, stomach, intestines, kidneys, brains, bone marrow, skin, and heart before getting around to eating the tougher and less tasty muscle tissue. It might be tempting to mistake these types of healthy, natural products with the by-products found in pet food. In fact, they are not the same.

Pet food by-products are often in the form of rendered meal. Rendering is the process of taking not-fit-for-human consumption foods and boiling them down to release the fat, which then floats to the top of the soupy mixture in the boiling vat. The fat is rendered off the top. Unfortunately, this separated fat is the most nutritionally valuable part of the food! After the fat is gone, the water is boiled and drained away and the protein, bones, and other leftovers in the vat are dried. The dried sludge is finally ground up so finely that you only see a homogenous powder called meat and bone meal, or animal by-product meal. Hardly "Bon appetit!" Fortunately for you—but not for your pet—you can't see what else may be finely ground into the meal.

I want to add something specifically about cats: the idea that cats all thrive on fish is more a creation of human fancy than reality. Modern-day cats descended from desert animals. There's a reason the Egyptians worshipped cats: there were a lot of cats hanging around to keep the rats, mice, vermin, and poisonous snakes at bay. These cats were protecting the people and their food supply. The people and the cats developed a synergistic relationship.

It's highly unlikely that the ancestral feline diet included much fish and much more likely that ancient cats lived on a diet of rodents and vermin, including small reptiles like lizards and salamanders. It's true that many cats enjoy the taste of fish, but there's no reason to think that fish is somehow inherently more pleasing to a cat than any other animal food.

Also, it's important to remember that cats are obligate carnivores. They are not vegetarians. Their digestive systems are designed to process meat (animal protein). Their livers and kidneys are not designed to detoxify fruits, berries, vegetables, grasses, legumes, grains, starches, or any kind of sugars, sweeteners, or chemicals. In fact, you should never feed any food that lists sugar, MSG, or aspartame as ingredients (this really goes for dogs too!). Beware and read carefully! The FDA has now allowed these ingredients to be hidden from you and can be listed as "natural flavors." That's consumer and pet protection? They have zero nutritional value, and in the case of sugar or any flavorings, can contribute to obesity and all of its associated health problems. Diabetes is one of the deadliest diseases for cats (and dogs).

In general, here are my two best pieces of advice about cats:

- Don't try to impose your eating habits on your cat, and
- Don't try to compete with them intellectually.

What about those label claims?

The only other way to get information about the relative nutrition of any pet food is to look at the label claims. This is where things can get really confusing and even misleading. The sad truth is that it's nearly impossible to separate marketing hype from good science on most pet food packages.

You might see pet food labeled as premium or super premium. Typically, these products are supposed to be made with higher quality ingredients and less water and carbohydrates. They are usually more expensive, but because they pack a greater nutritional punch with every bite, you usually feed less to your animal so the cost evens out somewhat compared to mass-market or economy brands. They are still "pet food," which you would not eat or feed to your other children.

In recent years, some super premium pet foods have begun introducing organic pet foods, although as of 2013, these still represent less than 5 percent of the market. While there is no set definition for what "organic pet food" is, AAFCO has recognized the term "organic" and adopted the same rules for organic pet food production that the United States Department of Agriculture applies to human foods. In general, this means if you see a pet food labeled organic, it means the product was made using animal or vegetable-based ingredients that are GMO-free, raised and fed on pastures that have not been synthetically fertilized, and the animals are antibiotic- and hormone-free. Also, any plant products in the food, or that were fed to organically raised animals used for food, were grown without pesticides, synthetic or sewage-sludge fertilizers, are non-irradiated, and are GMO-free.

The organic label should not be confused with the natural label, which is also increasingly common in super-premium pet foods. Pet foods labeled natural do not contain artificial coloring, flavoring, or preservatives. They are preserved using natural canning methods (vacuum-packed) and naturally occurring antioxidants, such as vitamin E and vitamin C. It is possible for a product to be labeled natural but not organic because its ingredients don't meet the USDA standards for organic productions.

The next obvious question is: Are these pet foods superior? Is a super-premium, natural, organic pet food a better option for your pet?

The answer is a resounding yes! Just as you want to give your pet as much variation in their food as possible, you want to provide the highest quality ingredients, with the lowest level of contaminants and chemicals as possible. This is really the same thing that applies to your own family's diet and explains why organic human foods have skyrocketed in sales in recent years. Studies have shown that organically produced foods contain profoundly lower levels of pesticides and other agricultural chemicals—and when you consider that pet's bodies are typically much smaller than human bodies, it's even more important to reduce their exposure to agricultural chemicals.

Similarly, just as with humans, animals can be sensitive or allergic to the preservatives and synthetic dyes and chemicals found in pet food. Switching to an organic pet food will often clear up skin and coat conditions, ease breathing and respiratory problems, and overall improve the health of your animal, without the need for antibiotics and steroids.

Organic is far superior to natural. Organic without sweetening or flavoring agents is the pinnacle of prevention. Understand this: If you add sugar, aspartame, or any other sweetener to the food, it may still be classified as "natural." This may be the rule to protect the industry, but it is potentially deadly to the animal that I took an oath to protect by swearing to: "First do no harm." The industry wants to sell pet food and the way to do it is to mix their stuff with sweeteners to hook the animal on it, just like they have done to us for three generations, increasing lucrative sales and profits for their families and stockholders.

There are a few other claims you might see on pet food labels. These include:

- Complete and balanced: The "complete and balanced" label is an AAFCO-approved label that means the food meets the minimum AAFCO standards for providing a technically complete diet for all life stages. Remember that AAFCO standards themselves satisfy only the basic requirements for nutrition—it is not an optimal diet, but only a satisfactory one. It is like saying, "All you ever need"—it might be psychologically satisfying, but it is also an empty buzzword and a non-scientific cliché.

- A limited claim: Limited claims are typically used to address different life stages. For example, a food might be labeled as "for adult dogs"

or "maintenance." These products have been formulated to meet the needs of animals in the different stages of life, so typically contain less fat,
protein, and other high-powered nutrients. They
often have more carbs and are cheaper.

- Intermittent or supplemental feeding only: This
  means the food should not be relied upon to provide a complete source of nutrition. Foods with
  this label will include treats, snacks, and other
  special-occasion foods. Instead, try a raw organic
  carrot for your dog!

- Therapeutic feeding only: These foods are typically
  labeled "use only as directed by your veterinarian."
  Supposedly designed to meet specific nutritional
  needs for animals under the care of a doctor, you
  should not feed one of these foods to your animals
  unless instructed to do so by your veterinarian (who

hopefully has read the label and understands what he or she is really giving you for your pet).

- Functional foods: The last category of label claims include the functional food claims. These are the health-related claims, such as "improves joint performance," "prevents hairballs," "fights tartar and plaque," and "good for your pet's coat." These claims are often made based on the presence of certain nutrients, such as glucosamine and chondroitin, omega-3 fatty acids, and others.

This can be a murky area. Legally speaking, all of these ingredients are classified as foods, as opposed to drugs. This means manufacturers can make general health claims but not medical claims. For example, "supports healthy joints" is considered a general health claim so it is allowed on labels. However, the claim "reduces inflammation" is a specific medical claim and would thus not be allowed on a pet food label.

The key difference is that general health claims do not have to be supported by the same kind of supposedly rigorous science and regulatory oversight as medical claims. In fact, while there is good data to support some of the functional food health claims made on labels, there is scant or questionable data on others. We'll discuss pet supplementation in greater depth in Chapter 7, but here are a few claims that are backed up by studies:

- Joint protection and glucosamine and chondroitin. There is a reason many veterinarians recommend these two supplements for animals with osteoarthritis and other joint disorders: high-quality studies have suggested they do support joint health by reducing cartilage breakdown. However, you should only use the proven glucosamine sulfate (not hydrochloride) and chondroitin sulfate.

- Joint protection and green-lipped mussel powder and UC-II collagen. Once again, studies have shown that these do aid in preventing joint deterioration and can help protect an animal suffering joint discomfort.

- Healthy coats and omega-3 and omega-6 fatty acids. We discussed this earlier, but there is good science showing that providing a correct balance of omega-3 and omega-6 fatty acids can improve your pet's coat and skin.

- Gastrointestinal health and probiotics. This is a very exciting area of research, with scores of human studies and increasing numbers of animal studies showing that probiotics can indeed improve digestive health. Probiotics are beneficial bacteria that live in the gut and aid in digestion and absorption.

They have also been shown to improve coat health
and shine, and boost immunity.

- Coat health and vitamin B. Although there isn't
a tremendous amount of data, some studies
have shown that various forms of vitamin B can
improve skin and coat health.

This is by no means an exhaustive list, but if you do see a
label claim with any of these nutrients, you can be more
confident that it's based on sound science. Understand,
however, there is no single product that does everything.
It is wise instead to use the best foundational food you can,
and then use supplements to control hairballs, improve
joint health, or control tartar. An optimal diet, following
my paradigm, will automatically produce healthy joints and
a beautiful coat, which is simply a reflection of the overall
health of the animal. This is what my paradigm is all about.

The most important message to take from this chapter is how crucial it is to understand what's in your pet's food.

Pet owners need to understand that the nutritional panel and label on your pet's food does give you valuable information, but you have to know how to read it. Many of the claims made on pet food labels have specific meanings behind them, and some of the things that owners focus on are not the most important part of the label.

As a pet parent, you owe it to your animal to first learn how to read the labels on your companion's food so you can make an informed decision and give your pet the highest quality, best food. The secret to reading a can or package of pet food is to:

- Look for the amount of moisture content. It's listed on all pet food containers as guaranteed analysis, but not with the other ingredients.

- Don't be fooled by ingredients that go by ＿＿ .e than one name, such as gluten meal, wheat, whole grain meal, and peas, pea protein, pea fiber, etc.

- Learn how to identify "good" types of protein versus TVP or certain types of by-products, such as lungs, tendons, skin, and rawhide.

- Determine the nutrient density and variety from the Nutrition Facts panel:

- Ingredient list

- Guaranteed analysis

- Count the percent of Protein, Fat, Fiber, Ash (minerals) and deduct those from 100 and you will find the astonishing amounts of carbs.

Once you've figured this out, you'll be well on your way to having the knowledge necessary to provide your animal with a healthy, lifelong diet.

# WHAT TO LOOK FOR WHEN
# READING PET FOOD LABELS

- Look at the ingredients in the food.

- Notice that the first ingredient is usually a wet ingredient in a dry food. This ingredient is the first by weight, but when it comes out of the extruder, it is the fourth, fifth, or sixth, because it has lost its water weight.

- Notice how much is meat (animal) and how much is carbohydrate (vegetable) and is it real meat or rendered meat meal?

- Understand what rendered is.

- Where is the protein? Is it from meat or from peas, or potato protein?

- If you add up the amounts of peas, pea fiber, pea protein, and pea starch, they may end up in the top of the ingredient list. That would be okay if your animal were a "pea-a-vore," but not if your animal is a carn-i-vore and CERTAINLY not if you are the parent or guardian of an OBLIGATE CARNIVORE cat.

- Are there peas and carrots, yucca, alfalfa, beans, corn, tapioca, potato, "natural flavors," and other toxic veggies in your cat's food?

# CHAPTER FIVE

# Canine Nutrition: Meeting Your Dog's Dietary Needs

WHEN CONSIDERING FEEDING YOUR DOG, IT CAN be helpful to understand how dogs have evolved and what they naturally eat. This can be a little difficult in regard to dogs, because they have been domesticated for so long (we think about twelve thousand years!) Instead, it helps to look at their closest living relatives: the wolves.

Contrary to what many people think, dogs and wolves are not true carnivores. In fact, dogs are omnivorous carnivores, whereas cats are obligate carnivores. Eating is mainly a pack activity, with a pack of hungry wolves gorging themselves quickly on a fresh kill and gulping down large quantities of food. Once full, hoarding behavior is relatively common, with animals burying bones and pieces of flesh to dig up and eat later, as my Corgi dog Bambi (pictured at the beginning of this chapter) does… yuck! In between these large meals, wolves might feed on grass, bark, berries, and other plant material.

Vestiges or signs of these ancient behavioral patterns can still be seen in modern dogs. For many dogs, eating too fast is a real problem—it can lead to choking or swallowing air that can lead to bloat and torsion of the stomach and intestinal tract. Similarly, some solitary dogs are known to eat too slow or too little. It's not uncommon for an owner to remark that their first dog was a "poor eater" right up until a second dog was introduced, then the "poor eater" became a normal eater. This is likely due to the old communal and competitive eating instinct kicking in.

It's also not uncommon for dogs to eat things that seem more than a little disgusting. Dogs (and wolves) are great scavengers and many dogs eat feces (called caprophagia). This behavior is not a symptom of any underlying problem. It's best to discourage both scavenging and eating poop because it is not sanitary and could pose a health risk to the dog's human companions, especially those dogs that are constantly licking your face. If you have a horse, then "Fugettaboutit!" Dogs love horse poop and there is no stopping them.

## IDEAL NUTRITION FOR EVERY STAGE OF LIFE

Just like humans, your dog's nutritional needs will change throughout the animal's life. A dog's energy needs, nutrient needs, and specific macronutrient needs, will change depending on whether the dog is pregnant or lactating, a growing puppy, an adult dog seeking to maintain good health, or an older dog in his or her golden years that is experiencing reduced appetite and possible nutritional deficiencies.

It also will depend on the breed: small and toy breed puppies don't grow nearly as quickly as the giant breeds like mastiffs and Great Danes, which can pack on over a hundred pounds of weight. In the same general time frame, a Chihuahua will gain only five or six pounds. Ideally, you should match your feeding habits to your dog's breed and stage of life. That being said, if you feed an optimal diet to any age or breed, you can bring the animal to a healthier and longer life.

## FEEDING PUPPIES: GIANT BREEDS VS. SMALL AND TOY BREEDS

No matter which breed you have, it's crucial to lay the groundwork for health during puppyhood. Unless you're very confident in your feeding program, I frequently recommend that owners give their puppy a supplement to complement their food. We'll discuss supplements in greater depth later, but for now, you should know that supplementation can prevent issues like hip dysplasia and elbow dysplasia, followed by arthritis later in life.

In fact, I believe so strongly in supplementation that, decades ago, I developed a pair of "superfood" supplements containing chelated minerals, digestive enzymes, probiotics, and antioxidants. The supplements are called Super-Food and Phyto-Food, followed by Superfood Antioxidant Boost and Superfood Immunopower, and made so you can sprinkle them onto your puppy's food. These two supplements have worked together for four decades to offset mistakes in feeding any breed of any size. Together, these will provide a serious nutrient boost. Believe it or not, over the past thirty-five years, I've never diagnosed a single case of hip or elbow dysplasia in dogs that have been raised using my supplements and following my eating protocols. In fact, preventing these common diseases has saved their pet parents countless thousands of dollars per dog in medical and surgical bills. But more than that, they have helped the pets to prevent the illnesses in the first place.

## FEEDING ADULT DOGS

No matter which breed, by the time your dog is six to eight months of age, the rapid growth of puppyhood is ending. For giant breeds, this time period might stretch out to a year or so, but it won't go much past that.

When growth stops, your dog's energy needs will typically be cut in half and their caloric need will decrease. In this stage of life, you should lower the amount of puppy food. Unfortunately, this is where many owners make the critical mistake of feeding their adult dogs carbs. As a result, between 20 and 60 percent of adult dogs in the United States are obese or overweight.

Since most dogs will spend the majority of their lives in this stage, it's critical to get the feeding right from the beginning. Instead of giving your dog access to endless quantities of carbohydrate-laden foods that suck up water and are quickly converted to sugar (and contain only the lowest levels of nutrients, keeping the dog hungry), it's a better approach to pick a very high-quality, nutrient-dense food that offers a wide variety of protein sources and minimal processed grains, potatoes, and starch. This will keep their blood sugar more stable, reduce hunger, and lower the risk of obesity.

Switching to a protein-rich food doesn't mean you should cut your dog off from the plant world entirely: if you want to give your dog carbohydrates, add half a baked sweet potato (never microwaved) to the food bowl every day. Sweet potatoes are packed with antioxidants, which support healthy immune function and reduce inflammation, and they (the potato skins) contain a natural source of fiber. You can also add any vegetables that your family has "left over" from dinner.

If you really want to amp up the nutrition profile of your dog's meal, you can follow a Paradigm I've developed over the years. When coupled with a premium, organic, natural food, the following feeding paradigm will help your adult dog be healthier and live longer. The steps are simple:

- Drizzle a little of my special olive oil over your dog's food to provide a great source of monounsaturated fatty acids;

- Add a sprinkle of my raw, high-quality Himalayan mountain crystal salt for an extra boost of more than eighty natural minerals;

- Supplement with my pair of superfood supplements, according to the label directions.

- Add my pure, organic sulfur (MSM) to the water bowl.

This feeding paradigm represents a potent health- and life-giving diet for adult dogs. It will help your dog's immune system fight and prevent diseases such as: diabetes, heart disease, kidney, and liver disease. It will also help to protect the health of your dog's gums and teeth, give them a bright, shiny coat, and will help your dog live to a very healthy, old age.

As your dog moves from adulthood into his or her senior years, you'll notice many of the same things happening with your dog that affect aging humans. Aging dogs lose muscle mass, gain fat weight, suffer from joint breakdown, and have reduced immune function and lower energy. They also have a naturally reduced appetite. At this stage in life, it's even more important to control the portions and carbs you're giving to your dog to reduce the risk of obesity.

You should continue to feed your older dog a high-quality, protein-dense food and maintain a regular exercise program, even if your dog doesn't have the same energy he or she used to have. Continue feeding lots of green vegetables and use the supplements for life. Make sure to get your veterinary check-ups! That means seeing your dog's doctor every six months.

## COMMON QUESTIONS FROM DOG OWNERS

### How much should my dog eat?

This is probably the most common question pet owners ask in my practice—and for good reason! Nobody wants an obese dog, because an obese dog is not a healthy dog. The idea that your dog isn't getting enough to eat is horrible. So how do you know? Let me explain.

The fundamental goal of feeding is to provide your dog with enough calories to meet the animal's energy needs. But this really only represents the beginning. Ideally, you want to provide your dog with a healthy diet full of varied, nutrient-dense ingredients that will allow your dog to thrive. This is where your choice of dog food comes in. A super-premium food with organic, all-natural ingredients will give your animal everything it needs without all those extra carb calories found in cheaper pet foods. In other words, the better quality of your food, the fewer cans and cups you'll need to provide for your dog—and the healthier your dog will be.

It's also important to keep in mind that your dog's calorie requirements will change throughout the animal's life. Dogs that are still growing, very active, or pregnant and lactating will require more real, organic food, while older dogs that are more sedentary will require less real, organic food.

Use your common sense. If the dog is getting skinny, then feed more real, organic food. If your dog is getting fat, feed less real, organic food. Are you getting this? The key to life in this twenty-first century is a diet that is completely and not partially organic!

### Should I "keep the bowl full" at all times?

The short answer is no.

When it comes to feeding your dog, there are three basic methods: free feeding, portion-controlled feeding, and time-controlled feeding. Free feeding means giving your dog access to food at all times throughout the day, so the animals can self-regulate their own food supply.

There are certain conditions in which free feeding is a good idea. For example, if your dog has very high energy needs (such as a working dog) or cannot eat very much at one time because of a medical condition, then giving your dog access to food all day might be a good idea.

Similarly, if you have many dogs that fight and bark during controlled feeding, it can make your life easier to simply provide unrestricted access to food. It might also be better to just separate the dogs to stop the stress of competition for food. Imagine yourself in that kind of situation. By the way, don't complain about your dog's table manners. They will wait quietly for leftovers until dinner is over. Speaking of table manners, they certainly won't be talking on their cell phones or texting during dinner.

However, for most dogs, free feeding is an invitation to obesity. It's not that dogs can't regulate their own caloric needs—in fact, many animals are very good at regulating their own food intake. But let's face it: it can be a lot to expect from a dog that leads basically a sedentary life, gets minimal exercise, and has unfettered access to very tasty food all day. Among these "couch potato" animals, obesity is a real problem, along with all the health issues that come with it. Think of what you would look like if you spent your life on a cruise ship with an endless buffet.

### Should my dog eat more or less during winter? What about during summer?

With extreme weather becoming more frequent (thank you HAARP), it's common for owners to wonder if very hot or very cold weather will affect their dog's appetite and caloric need. The answer is yes! Dogs have evolved to be protected from cold weather by increasing their body temperature, which naturally requires more calories. In fact, some studies have shown that dogs in the Arctic have an increased caloric need of 70 to 80 percent over dogs in more temperate environments. Overall, during times of extreme cold, you might expect to see dogs increase their food intake by about 25 percent. Keep in mind that your dog's coat length can affect this also: dogs with longer (and thicker) coats are better protected from the cold.

### *What about heat?*

Many people are surprised to learn that their dog's caloric needs will also increase during extreme heat. It's not as dramatic for dogs in cold weather, but in some ways it can be more dangerous. Dogs in very hot weather have increased caloric needs to help cool the body—yet many dogs have a reduced appetite when they are too hot. Don't be surprised to see them eating more during hot spells. If they are not If the dog is not, however, look out for unexpected weight loss and alert your pet's doctor if you see anything unusual.

In addition, many dogs don't drink enough during hot weather and in times of increased physical activity. For their health, it's essential to make sure that they are getting enough filtered water and nutrient-dense food during a heat wave. This is another good reason for a great can of real, organic human-grade food.

### Is chocolate really deadly for dogs?

Yes! Chocolate contains a chemical called theobromine that is toxic for dogs. Although toxicology studies are rare, it is estimated that a dose of about 100mg/kg (100 mg for each 2.2 lbs. or 1 gram for each 22 lbs.) of body weight is enough to cause serious toxicity in dogs.

A dog that has consumed too much theobromine will usually begin to show symptoms of toxicity within four or five hours. Symptoms include: vomiting, uncontrolled urination, panting, diarrhea, and tremors. If you see these symptoms in your dog and suspect that he or she recently ate chocolate, seek out medical help immediately.

Chocolate is not the only food that is toxic for dogs. There are actually many more foods that are toxic: grapes, raisins, macadamia nuts, onions, garlic, alcohol, bread, coffee, and tea are all purported to be toxic for dogs. Xylitol, found in sugarless chewing gum, is deadly! Don't give this stuff to them and they will be okay! Other than garlic, which is eaten by dogs every night around the world via the leftovers of their Mediterranean heritage parents, you wouldn't have given these things anyway. It is just common sense. Remember that sugar, sugar substitutes, and aspartame are also toxic to dogs—as well as being toxic to people. Check with your veterinarian before feeding any food item if you are unsure of its safety.

In an emergency involving the ingestion of a toxic substance, call the national poison control hotline at 1-800-222-1222.

# CHAPTER SIX

# Feline Nutrition: Meeting Your Cat's Dietary Needs

IF DOGS ARE LIKE THE PICK-UP TRUCKS OF THE PET world, think of cats like Ferraris. As tempting as it can be to lump cats and dogs into the same category as "companion animals," they are very different species with different and unique nutritional requirements.

Cats are obligate carnivores. They do not need vegetables. Cats must eat meat, including: fish, eggs, beef, lamb, lizards, reptiles, crickets, birds, rodents, etc. They rarely eat any plant material (although catnip could be an obvious exception). As a result, cat food typically contains more animal protein and meat than dog food but should not contain carbohydrate fillers.

This diet, however, is necessary for cats because of the way they evolved. The modern housecat likely evolved from a desert species of cats in northern Africa. Ancestral cats were strict carnivores, and they developed a number of unique dietary needs to compensate for the lack of plant material in their environment. This is especially important for pet owners who are vegans and believe in feeding their animals a plant-based diet. This should not be done.

There are three main requirements that are unique to a cat's diet:

***Higher protein requirements.*** Cats have a higher protein requirement for every pound of body weight than dogs. While it's hard to be too precise with a general recommendation—cats' protein requirements depend on the size of the animal, stage in life, activity level, and other factors—a high-quality dry cat food should be at least 30 percent animal protein. Also, there is a widespread misconception that excess protein in an adult cat's diet will result in kidney disease. You should know there is no research backing up this claim. Older cats should not be on a protein-restricted diet, but should continue to be supplied with plenty of animal protein with a high biological value (not by-products), such as muscle and glandular meat—not tendons, lungs, rawhide, TVP (textured vegetable protein), meat by-products, soybean meal, meat and bone meal, or any other meal that has been made with vegetation, including pea protein and corn protein. No potato protein!

***Supplemental arachidonic acid.*** Arachidonic acid is a polyunsaturated fatty acid that has many important functions in the body, including contributing to immune system and circulatory health. Many mammals have developed the ability to convert other dietary fats into arachidonic acid, but this ability is reduced in cats. As a result, cats deficient in arachidonic acid can develop blood problems, such as reduced clotting and having smaller litters of kittens, and they can also develop an overall weakening in their protective immune system. It's important to ensure that your cat is getting enough arachidonic acid from its diet, or at least adequate linoleic acid, which is converted into arachidonic acid.

There is an important caution here, however. Many cat owners are led to believe they can increase their cat's levels of healthy fats by adding vegetable oil (which is another source of linoleic acid). Unless you're able to do the kind of advanced food analysis a pet nutrition lab can perform, this is a bad idea. In all likelihood, adding vegetable oil to your cat's food will create an imbalance between the various kinds of fats and essential fatty acids and provide higher-than-optimal levels of omega-6 fatty acids. This can lead to an inflammatory condition called pansteatitis.

Pansteatitis is a vitamin E deficiency affecting various mammals, primarily cats, that are fed excess omega-3 polyunsaturated fatty acids from fish oils, particularly tuna. This can also occur when feeding omega-6 polyunsaturated fatty acids from vegetable oil. In cats, pansteatitis causes inflammation of all fat tissues, turning the cat's fat yellow. This is why it is known as yellow fat disease. Since all animal fats contain arachidonic acid, give your cat a real food rich in animal fats, not one containing vegetable oil. Animal fat is more expensive. That's a good thing. Everything that is better is more expensive.

COMPASSION FOR PETS | DR. R. GEOFFREY BRODERICK, DVM

Some pet food manufacturers like to add canola oil, which is made from genetically modified rapeseed oil. The rape plant produces the seed from which the oil is derived. Who buys oil in the supermarket? Women do! What woman is going to go and ask the stock-boy where the rape oil is located? No woman! Rapeseed is grown in Canada, hence the marketing "boys club" came up with the name, canola. Canola oil is toxic to cats. Don't feed it to them.

***Supplemental taurine.*** Taurine is an amino acid, or protein building block. It is considered an essential amino acid for cats as they cannot make taurine in their bodies and must get it from their food. Taurine deficiency in cats can cause a host of problems, especially a heart condition called cardiomyopathy. This occurs when the heart muscle becomes weak and flaccid and the heart can no longer pump efficiently. As recently as twenty years ago, taurine deficiency was a major cause of heart problems in cats. Since pet food manufacturers were told that adding supplemental taurine to the cat's diet reduces the risk of cardiomyopathy, the number of cases caused by taurine deficiency has dropped dramatically, but it can still be an issue with lower-quality foods.

***Supplemental preformed vitamin A.*** Unlike dogs, cats lack the enzyme that converts dietary carotenoids into vitamin A, which makes sense considering that carotenoids are primarily found in orange colored vegetables and cats are carnivores. This doesn't mean cats don't need vitamin A, however. In fact, it makes it more important to supply a dietary source of vitamin A.

Fortunately, high levels of preformed vitamin A can be found in liver and liver oil, which are both common ingredients in quality cat food. If your cat is deficient in vitamin A, the animal will suffer from poor bone growth and neurological disorders.

# IDEAL NUTRITION FOR EVERY
# STAGE OF YOUR CAT'S LIFE

## Feeding Kittens

Because they're growing rapidly, kittens have higher energy requirements than their lazier and larger adult counterparts. This requirement for extra energy peaks around five weeks of age. Depending on the cat, you can expect a twelve-week-old kitten weighing about two pounds to need ½ cup (4 oz. or 2 oz. per lb.) of food per day. This assumes, of course, that you're using high-quality, protein-rich, high-animal-fat food.

As your cat continues to grow, the cat will need less energy per pound of body weight—but this will be offset by the fact that your adult cat will weigh more than a kitten, so therefore will consume more food overall. In general, an adult seven-month-old (thirty weeks) cat will only need half as many calories per pound of body weight as a kitten (about 1 oz. per lb.), but it will likely weigh more than three times as much as a kitten, so your adult cat will eat a greater overall quantity of food than your kitten (about 6-8 oz.). Feed kittens all they want, at least four to six times per day (every four to six hours). Eight times is even better.

## Feeding Adult Cats

Adult cats are relatively easy to feed. Most adult cats will self-regulate their own food intake with no problem, whether it is dry or canned food. Dry food should be kept in an airtight container to prevent it from getting stale. If you feed your adult cat a high-quality canned food, don't worry if it doesn't finish the whole can at one sitting. Cats are more frequent eaters, so there's nothing wrong with your cat eating a little, then letting it sit for a while to come

## AVOIDING PET ALLERGENS

ONE OF THE MAJOR CAUSES OF DISEASE IS AN unhealthy gut or digestive tract. Don't give something that causes diarrhea. If your body rejects something or reacts negatively to it, or has a craving for it (like sugar), you are probably allergic to it. The same thing goes for our pets.

back for more. Canned food is cooked, so you don't have to worry about surface bacteria growing on it like you would with raw food. Don't push it, though—canned food can get stale after a while so leave it in a cool place (never in the sun) for a limited time and portion out the servings. Make sure that the can is covered with a plastic lid or airtight seal. Cats are generally not bothered by other cats eating from the same bowls or platters.

## COMMON QUESTIONS FROM CAT OWNERS

### *How often should I feed my cat?*

This is an excellent question—and one that many pet owners get wrong if they try to logic it out. It's tempting to think of cats as smaller versions of their wild cousins, tigers and lions. If you've ever watched a nature special on TV, you know that these large predatory cats are accustomed to going for long periods of time without food, then gorging themselves on a fresh kill, which will hold them over until they eat again.

Domestic cats don't follow this pattern, under normal circumstances. Instead, most housecats will easily fall into the pattern of the small, wild cats they descended from, which means eating many small meals throughout the day. It is thought this pattern closely mimics the hunting patterns of ancestral cats: they would catch and consume small rodents and reptiles throughout the day, but never bring down large prey. As a result, cats with free access to food will tend to nibble all day long, sometimes having as many a dozen "meals" throughout the day, with each "meal" consisting of as little as twenty calories. Unless you are feeding highly palatable food that cats are likely to overeat, and your cat gets plenty of exercise, it's acceptable to leave food out for your cats to eat at will through the day. If, however, you have an indoor cat with little or no exercise, you'll have to control portions to prevent obesity.

### Can I feed my cat tuna from the can?

As I have said, housecats descended from desert animals, which means that ancestral cats probably didn't have much access to fish—but there's also no question that cats seem to love the taste of fish. As a result, many owners think they are doing their cats a favor by giving them tuna from the can.

You should be aware, however, that this practice can actually cause serious health problems for your cat. Tuna packed in oil contains very high levels of polyunsaturated omega-6 fatty acids. A certain amount of this type of fat is necessary for your cat, but too much of it can cause a disease known as pansteatitis. This condition is linked to a vitamin E deficiency, which itself is caused by eating too much polyunsaturated fatty acids that promote inflammation in the body. As a major antioxidant, vitamin E is used to reduce the inflammation—until the cat's body no longer has enough vitamin E and develops pansteatitis. The oil in the tuna can is not supplemented with vitamin E unless it says so.

COMPASSION FOR PETS | DR. R. GEOFFREY BRODERICK, DVM

## *Is milk OK for an adult cat?*

There's no doubt kittens love milk—people have been leaving saucers of milk out for hungry kittens for as long as there have been saucers and milk. It can be tempting to assume that milk would also be a treat for an adult cat... but giving too much milk to an adult cat can lead to some unpleasant cleaning up.

Milk has a type of sugar called lactose. In the body, lactose is broken down by the enzyme lactase. Kittens (and puppies) have high levels of lactase, making it easy for them to break down lactose. A cat's mother's milk is about 5 percent lactose. However, after they're weaned and as they grow, the cat's production of lactase declines and, just like many people, they can become lactose intolerant. Adult cats that are lactose intolerant will experience diarrhea if they consume too much milk, so as a general rule, it's a good idea to lay off the milk for most adult cats.

*I'm a vegetarian. Is it OK to raise a vegetarian cat?*

The first question you should ask yourself is why you want to raise a vegetarian cat in the first place. People are vegetarian for a variety of reasons, including moral, dietary, and religious reasons. It's important to remember that none of these reasons apply to cats, which have evolved as carnivores and thrive on a diet comprised almost exclusively of animal proteins and fats. Please don't try to impose unnatural restrictions on your cat. Another caveat to the vegetarian cat is that you cannot ever let it out in the yard. It does not understand your reasoning and will devour the first critter it can get its paws on.

*My vet says my cat is overweight. Is this a serious problem?*

Yes! Along with diabetes and cancer, obesity is one of the leading killers of domestic cats. Many cats don't get much physical activity and have access to a continuous buffet of delicious, highly caloric foods full of carbs and "natural flavors," which entice the animal to overeat. Remember that sugar, aspartame, and MSG are all classified as "natural."

The cat does not want or need carbs, which produce insulin that takes glucose out of the blood and locks it into fat cells. Each pound of stored fat holds about nine pounds of water, adding ten pounds to the cat, doubling its weight, slowing it down, and making it a sick, lazy couch potato.

When the cat eats protein, it triggers the release of glucogon instead of insulin from the pancreas. Glucogon unlocks the fat cells to transform the high-caloric fat into glucose at an even pace and delivers it to the cat's brain, liver, and muscle when needed to catch its prey. Now we have the long, sleek, healthy cat back who can run fast and climb any tree. Now we also have a cat that has a greater chance of living a longer, healthier life free of diabetes.

### *Why does my cat need so many more meals than my dog?*

A cat's entire digestive system is only about 40% (less than half) of the digestive system of a dog weighing the same amount. Cats digest and eliminate their food faster than dogs. The domestic cat evolved from the desert cat, who was designed to eat small and frequent meals 24/7.

# CHAPTER SEVEN

# Dietary Supplements for Pets: Necessary or Not?

DIETARY SUPPLEMENTS ARE A BOOMING BUSINESS FOR people—but the idea of dietary supplements for animals is still relatively new. A few pioneering veterinarians like myself have developed comprehensive supplement formulas. I created my Cornucopia Super-Food and Phyto-Food for pets in the 1970s, and now Superfood Antioxidant Boost and Superfood Immunopower are being introduced. It's only recently that big-name pet food companies have gotten into the market.

Perhaps because of their large marketing budgets, and perhaps because of people's overall comfort with supplementation, this area of the pet food market is growing quickly, especially if you include the so-called "functional foods" in the overall picture. Functional foods are food products, including pet food itself, that have been fortified with a dietary supplement. The classic example is dog food that has been fortified with glucosamine and chondroitin. Most of the big, new products work at questionable levels, but it gets the Big Pharma companies into the game.

First off, it's helpful to understand what dietary supplements are exactly and who is responsible for their safety. In the most general terms, there are three classes of substances you might give an animal:

- Food
- Dietary supplements
- Animal drugs

Food itself is obviously not a dietary supplement, even if you're giving your pet some type of human food or special treat. Most pet nutritionists will tell you that a healthy, balanced diet is all you need to keep your animals healthy, and that pet supplements are an unnecessary extravagance. Now we are back to the old cliché that "complete and balanced is all you ever need." This is true to a degree—but it depends on the quality of your pet's diet. If you're giving your cat or dog a super-premium, natural, organic pet food (and for dogs, adding nutrient-packed foods like sweet potato, olive oil, and mineral-rich salt), then it's likely you are delivering an optimal diet for your animal. Remember, though, that many pet foods are not designed to provide optimal nutrition and they are also not truly organic. They have been formulated to provide the AAFCO-approved minimum levels of nutrients just to keep your animal alive.

This is where dietary supplements come in. Dietary supplements are additional nutrients, including vitamins and minerals, that are used to fortify an animal's diet. As we learn more and more about optimal animal nutrition, the need for dietary supplements for many animals is becoming clear. Also, supplements should be cold manufactured in a powdered form, where they are not subjected to heat. The heat in food processing, as well as the encapsulation process and the making of the tablets, kills a lot of the nutrients. A wide variety of other nasty ingredients are added to pills and tablets, some of which include:

- Fillers: lactose, microcrystalline cellulose, corn starch, sugars, whey, maltodextrin
- Binders: povidone, Carbopol
- Disintegrants: crospovidone, croscarmelose sodium, gellan gum

- Coatings: shellac
- Lubricants, colorants, flavors, and plasticizers: magnesium stearate, stearic acid, sodium stearyl fumarate, hydrogenated oil, polyethylene glycol, titanium dioxide, iron oxides

You don't need these added ingredients in powders. That's why we make our supplements in powder form.

First, it's important to understand that many ingredients in high-powered supplements may not be on the list of AAFCO-recommended nutrients. The reason for this is that AAFCO does not have the resources (money and people power) to research every wonderful ingredient that Mother Nature has provided. For example, many of the ingredients I use are found in exotic places around the world, where native, aboriginal people have used them for scores of centuries in traditional medicine. We select

## BE CAREFUL OF DRUGS

**M**ORE AND MORE, WE ARE BEGINNING TO understand that antibiotics, steroids, and other drug-related side effects can wreak havoc with our animals.

only the highest quality ingredients, and then produce them using a cold-manufacturing process that preserves and protects the key nutrients.

Beyond supplements, there are the animal drugs. These substances are formulated to address specific health conditions in companion animals. They are regulated by the Food and Drug Administration (FDA) and prescribed by veterinarians. The key point to understand here is that animal drugs and supplements are very different in the way they are marketed and sold. Unlike drug makers, pet supplement manufacturers are not allowed to make specific health claims related to their products. For example, they cannot say, "Will cure psoriasis." Instead, the manufacturer can only make a statement of function, such as, "Can help support a healthy coat and skin."

However—and this is important—this is technically the law, but it is almost never enforced. The truth is, government agencies like the FDA have their hands full regulating the booming human pharmaceutical and supplement market; there are few resources left over to effectively regulate the pet supplement industry. As a result, there are unscrupulous companies marketing pet food supplements with medical claims that are not supported by scientific evidence. Unfortunately, this means buyers must beware. Only buy pet supplements from companies you trust or that have been recommended by a qualified veterinary nutritionist, or companies that make reasonable claims they can explain—if they will give you the time. When in doubt, it's always a good idea to ask your veterinary nutritionist. A veterinarian should be able to help you sort through the various ingredients and label claims, but in general, veterinarians and physicians are not experts in nutrition.

## EXCITING SUPPLEMENT RESEARCH

The field of animal nutrition has made tremendous progress in the last few decades—including huge steps forward in the study of dietary supplements and how adding specific nutrients to your pet's diet can make a big difference in their quality of life. From a veterinarian's perspective, it's exciting to see the field of animal health and welfare finally beginning to catch up with—and in some cases surpass—the tremendous progress made in human health, especially in the functional-alternative-medicine area.

Here are some of the more exciting areas of research:

*Probiotics.* Some of the most exciting research in the field of preventive medicine is taking place with probiotics. Simply put, probiotics are "friendly bacteria" that live in the gut. There are many strains of probiotic bacteria. A couple of the most well-known are Bifidobacterium and Lactobacillus. They are responsible for a variety of functions, including healthy digestion, absorption of nutrients, maintaining a healthy coat, and promoting a healthy immune system.

An increasing number of scientific studies in dogs and cats show that probiotics can help prevent illness in animals by boosting immune function and maintaining a healthy gut pH and flora. *Properly managing the intestinal health in cats and dogs, as well as all domestic animals, can prevent toxic bacterial overgrowth. You cannot have a healthy, powerful, aggressive and defensive immune system without a healthy digestive system (gut).*

Wild animals are not fed by people. They are natural, aboriginal hunters and gatherers that find and eat the needed variety of different foods on their own. Wild and organic foods contain probiotics found in nature. When these foods are subjected to chemical pesticides, fertilizers, and antibiotics, they can lose their probiotic properties. *We must return to an organic way of life to prevent the spiral of sickness and decreasing longevity.*

*Antioxidants.* Antioxidants are a class of molecules that prevent inflammation throughout the body. A good way to think of antioxidants is to think of them like a sponge: antioxidants are capable of "soaking up," or neutralizing, harmful molecules and chen

been linked to inflammation. In turn, inflammation has

been linked to the development of cancer, heart disease,

arthritis, diabetes, and numerous other diseases associ-

ated with aging.

The most well-known antioxidants are vitamin C, vitamin A (carotinoids), vitamin E, zinc, selenium, and compounds known as polyphenols, which are abundant in colorful plants. In the 1970s, Dr. Wendell Bellfield and I worked under the guidance of two-time Nobel Prize winner, Dr. Linus Pauling, using vitamin C to prevent hip dysplasia in dogs. We found that although dogs make their own vitamin C, it becomes depleted during periods of stress, such as being taken away from their mothers and siblings, being put in a new environment, getting vaccinated, or being sick. When vitamin C production drops, the cells lining the joints are malformed and the process of hip dysplasia begins. When we supplemented animals with vitamin C, they failed to get hip dysplasia. In fact, there hasn't been a single case of hip dysplasia in either of our practices among clients who followed our instructions in the use of vitamin C. We did this work four decades ago and still the veterinary profession holds on to the erroneous assumption that hip dysplasia is a genetic disease, when it is not. Hip dysplasia is a nutritional disease caused by inadequate production of vitamin C during times of stress coupled with lack of adequate vitamin C in the diet.

In the 1970s, the Shute brothers of the Shute Institute in London, Ontario, Canada, told me of their fantastic results in heart disease with vitamin E. This information has been passed by me to a multitude of veterinarians, and we have all had success with vitamin E ever since. I once gave it to a nine-year-old Great Dane with terminal, debilitating, dilated cardiomyopathy. The dog died four years later in an accident at age thirteen, while chasing his parent's car for two blocks at a "full-cry."

Antioxidants have been shown to boost immunity and support pregnant and lactating animals, as they do in all animals. They do this by donating an electron to a destructive atom that is missing an electron. This wild atom is called a free radical, and it causes damage, as well as aging in the animal's body through a process called oxidation (losing an electron.) This is the same process that causes aluminum to oxidize or iron to rust in an old gate or a bridge (as in the aging and debilitated infrastructure of our great country) or a rubber band to lose its flexibility. Then, when the electron donor (antioxidant) gives the electron to the free radical, the free radical is neutralized (reduced to a normal atom) and no longer causes damage. This fantastic healing reaction occurs at the atomic and molecular level. This defense mechanism of the body, with the help of antioxidants, preserves the integrity of the cells at the cellular level. Healthy cells help prevent organs from getting sick. Healthy organs prevent the body from getting sick.

*Omega-3 fatty acids.* The omega-3 fatty acids act as antioxidants when they are circulating in the bloodstream. Speaking of circulating in the bloodstream, the omega-3 fatty acids happen to be the antifreeze of the fish because they keep the blood free-flowing and prevent it from getting thick and slowing down in cold and freezing water.

*Enzymes.* Enzymes are a special type of protein. They are used throughout the body to aid in a multitude of chemical reactions. Enzymes are both produced internally and consumed through the diet, depending on the enzyme. In recent years, an explosion of interest has put digestive enzymes for animals in the spotlight, and more and more veterinarians are recommending their usage.

As the name implies, digestive enzymes aid in the proper digestion of food. This is important for dogs and cats that are fed sub-optimal diets. Over time, their ability to produce adequate digestive enzymes declines, so instead of food being properly broken down in the gut, the food ferments (or rots). The result is poor nutrient absorption and possible health problems, including digestive problems from the toxins released by rotting food. Supplemental enzymes can help your pet more completely break down food, which increases nutrient absorption and has powerful health benefits, such as supporting a healthier immune system, improving coat appearance, reducing digestive upset, keeping teeth and gums healthy, and promoting better heart and joint health. Leaky gut "syndrome" is also a major cause of allergies and disease.

*Joint-supporting supplements.* Alongside probiotics, the joint-supporting supplements are some of the best-validated and most heavily recommended supplements for animals. There is a wealth of research showing that glucosamine and chondroitin can help prevent or slow joint disintegration among older animals, which reduces pain and improves mobility. They do this by attacking and reducing inflammation inside the joint, thus preserving and repairing the cushion of cartilage that helps lubricate and soften joints. It's not uncommon for a veterinarian to recommend a range of anti-inflammatory supplements for dogs (and cats) suffering from inflammatory joint pain, including: glucosamine and chondroitin, omega-3 fatty acids, the antioxidants vitamin E, vitamin C, selenium, and MSM (methylsulfonylmethane), a source of sulfur and a pain reducer. Green-lipped mussel, which has also shown promise in preventing joint pain, is a natural source of chondroitin. We supply the pure, organic sulfur (MSM) that works the best.

*Healthy coats.* Just like the gums and teeth, an animal's coat is an excellent indicator of overall health. A coat that is dull or patchy generally indicates an underlying health issue and may be one of the first signs of disease. In most cases, the underlying problem is dietary. The condition of an animal's coat can be a warning sign that the animal is deficient in some nutrient. One of the most common deficiencies leading to a lackluster coat is a lack of omega-3 fatty acids. This can occur for a number of reasons, including: insufficient digestive enzymes to aid in the digestion of fatty acids, a dietary lack of omega-3 fatty acids, and a low-fat diet mistakenly used for obese animals. If your animal has a poor quality coat, consider adding a high-quality source of omega-3 fatty acids to his or her diet. Symptoms of excess fatty acids include loose stools or diarrhea.

It's important to note that a poor coat can be related to a skin condition as well. For example, a simple flea or tick allergy, or a mange mite infestation, can cause your pet to claw at their skin, thus opening up sores or ripping out chunks of hair. Food sensitivities to substandard pet food ingredients can also cause "hot spots" of red, inflamed skin and baldness. If you suspect any of these causes, try to correct as many of these issues as you can. This might mean switching shampoo, treating for fleas or changing your flea treatment, and supplementing with high-quality skin-protecting nutrients like antioxidants and omega-3 fatty acids. Never underestimate the power of a good, real, organic food to improve skin and coat health! That alone could prevent most of these problems to begin with. Dissolve ¼ teaspoon of pure, organic sulfur (MSM) in the water bowl each time you change it.

***Circulatory health.*** Heart disease is unfortunately common in older dogs and taurine-deficient cats. Once again, the culprit is often a poor-quality food that has led to obesity or a nutrient deficiency that has finally weakened the heart. Remember, if your dog or cat suffers from heart disease or any heart condition, there is no substitute for the care of a competent veterinarian, and if they are suffering from any abnormal condition, ask your veterinarian about adding the following supplements to the pet's diet:

- **_Taurine._** Taurine deficiency is more common in cats, as taurine is an essential amino acid. However, with the advent of mass-produced, substandard foods that rely on textured vegetable protein and genetically modified soy, taurine deficiency and its related heart problems are becoming more common in dogs as well. Supplemental taurine, in the form of either a tablet or taurine-abundant raw meat, can help reverse this.

- *Carnitine.* Carnitine is an amino acid similar to taurine. It is found in high quantities in red meats, so it won't be surprising to learn that dogs fed inferior foods with vegetable proteins are more likely to suffer from a carnitine deficiency that causes heart problems. Carnitine deficiency can be corrected with supplements or by providing raw red meat. Do not use the synthetic forms of carnitine as they can cause side effects. Foods rich in carnitine are what carnivores evolved on: pure, organic meat and wild (antibiotic and GMO-free) fish.

- *Fish oil (omega-3 fatty acids).* This is where the omega-3 fatty acids really shine. These essential fatty acids have been conclusively shown to reduce inflammation in the heart and coronary arteries, as well as improve heart function and oxygen utilization. Even animals without heart disease will likely benefit from the addition of omega-3 fatty acids to their diet. If you are supplementing with omega-3 fatty acids, it's a good idea to provide a vitamin E supplement as well, because high levels of omega-3 fatty acids have been shown to reduce the availability of vitamin E. A diet containing fish as an ingredient will supply the needed and available animal-based omega-3 fatty acids on a constant and preventative basis. Fish is another food that carnivores evolved on. When I first formulated "Cornucopia" I started with fish. Now over 47 years later, fish is still a major ingredient in my organic foods.

Finally, it's important to think about something that many pet owners often overlook: sunlight. Sunlight is an essential "nutrient" in the sense that every function in your animal's body depends on sunlight. Your pet's ability to produce vitamin D3 is only one of them. Most dogs go for a walk a few times a day and receive the nourishing rays of the sun…but many do not. Cats and small dogs are increasingly locked inside homes and apartments with litter boxes and wee-wee pads without access to sunlight or fresh air. If you provide a sunny spot, they will use it. They intuitively will go to a place that is healthy for them. They must get SUN.

Make sure that a windowsill or a shelf is available to your animal to perch on to receive the sun and get a stimulating view of the outside world.

## THE LAST WORD ON PET SUPPLEMENTS

There's no question that very exciting things are happening in the world of pet supplements. There is wonderful research coming out every day validating the use of supplements for conditions ranging from poor coat quality, to heart disease, arthritis, and other conditions.

Remember, supplements should never be the foundation of your pet's healthy diet. The best approach to pet nutrition is to give your animal the very best food possible, which provides a rich and varied diet that closely resembles the animal's ancestral diet. Also, it's a good idea to check with your veterinary doctor before diagnosing any nutrient deficiency in your animal. In some cases, a simple blood test can give you some of the information you'll need. You may always get a second opinion from an experienced veterinary nutritionist, just as you would for yourself from visiting a human nutritionist. "Remember, you can't supplement s--t!" This old adage that uses a different word means that if the food is worthless or problematic to begin with, there is no reason to try to supplement it. Just stop using it, feeding it, or eating it. And since you would never, ever eat your pet's "pet food," your food immediately qualifies for the old adage.

# CHAPTER EIGHT

# Optimal Feeding

IF YOU TAKE ANY MESSAGE AWAY FROM THIS BOOK, IT will hopefully be this: your pet can survive on basic mass-marketed pet food, but there are much better options. Just like with human nutrition, the advances we've made in animal nutrition and health make it possible to design an optimal diet for your animal. The benefits of this are profound: less disease, better skin and coat, improved immunity, healthier animals, and an increased lifespan for your pets that is mind-blowing.

For many people, the road to optimal pet nutrition starts in the grocery store, where they've likely been buying the same kind of "pet food" without really thinking about it, simply because it's called "pet food." The next step is learning to read the labels and finding out what's really in pet food. People are surprised to learn that in most cases, pet foods made for obligate carnivores like cats or even omnivorous carnivores like dogs, are primarily made up of free water and cheap carbs. Finally, there is the education process, where people begin to learn what an optimal pet diet really looks like and how they can get the best food for their animals. This book is designed for just that purpose—to help you sort through the marketing claims and get to the truth underneath.

As a last thought, I wanted to close on a personal note. I've spent my life and career caring for animals. I've seen over a quarter of a million animals come through my clinic. I've seen countless thousands that suffered from allergies, skin conditions, ear infections, gum disease, kidney disease, liver disease, joint disease, heart disease, diabetes, cancer, and other disabling diseases. As I've worked with pet owners to clean up and improve their pets' diets, I've seen firsthand the incredible results of food as medicine. I've seen obese animals lose weight and cut their disease risk. I've seen animals with intractable food allergies regain their health, and I've seen animals improve their joint, heart, liver, and even eye health, all through the power of a healthy diet. I've seen my patients live a life free of ear infections and mouth infections. I have cured, controlled, and prevented urinary bladder infections and dissolved urinary bladder stones without surgery starting from the mid-1970s. This was the same era when my west coast partner and I eradicated hip dysplasia through preventive nutrition, while people, even until today, keep singing the same old song that (money-making) hip dysplasia is a non-preventable genetic disease. To quote my dear friend Irene deVilliers, "Man who say it can't be done should not interrupt one doing it."

My purpose in writing this book is to give you the information you need to make informed decisions about your pet's diet—and to show you that there really is incredible healing power in real, organic food. This is true for you, and it's also true for your pets. So don't throw out your healthy leftovers. Mix them into your pet's new food—which must be a human-grade, superb, real, pure organic food for pets. These leftovers will add endless variety to liven up your pet's real, organic diet.

Don't be frugal! Invest in your pet, who has given you the priceless gift of unconditional love. Pay it forward, and you will reap monetary returns as well, with fewer visits to the emergency room and the oncologist's office by using far less costly preventive health care instead of standard of sick care.

Think for a moment what you are doing. Would you eat this stuff? Would you give this to your other children? The only insurance for your pet is to feed real, pure, organic food, free of sweeteners, antibiotics, gluten, and GMOs and—the most recent stealth scam—"natural flavors," whatever they are.

# CHAPTER NINE

# Genetically Modified Organisms (GMOs)

THE DOMINANT TRAIT OF GM PLANTS IS HERBICIDE tolerance (HT). HT crops are genetically engineered to survive an otherwise toxic dose of a genetically modified weed killer, such as glyphosate. Genetic engineering is not sex or natural breeding, as has been done for millions of years, where both parents contribute thousands of genes to the offspring and acquire the trait of both in a natural way. In genetic engineering, only a single gene is removed from the DNA of an organism and forcibly inserted into another with questionable and unnatural results. A dog can mate with a dog, and an onion can be bred with an onion, but it is not possible for a dog to mate with an onion. But by using genetic engineering, anything is possible and the results defy Mother Nature.

Animals, such as pigs, geese, squirrels, elk, deer, raccoons, mice, and rats, have been observed to naturally avoid GM foods. Dogs and cats are lured into eating them by adding enticers, such as sugars, aspartame, MSG, and an array of harmful substances that can be labeled as "natural flavors." Some studies on genetic engineering suggest they may not be as safe as we have been led to believe! The process of gene insertion could be responsible for disrupting both our DNA and that of our pets.

When studies on GMO foods were finally done by renowned scientists, they found altered levels of nutrients and toxins that created disease, sickness, and death in controlled animal studies, as well as reported observations of negative reactions from GMOs. Those reporters and scientists were belittled, defamed, fired, boycotted, and removed from making a living. This created a gag order reaction for those who were opposed to GMOs and the biotech industry and they lived in fear of losing their jobs and lives.

Since that time, many accounts of sickness and death have leaked out, causing a mounting awareness of the scientific fact that genetic engineering is unscientific. Even the media has a gag order on it for fear of the withdrawal of advertising dollars by the GMO giants. Allergies have gone off the charts since GM crops and foods have been on the market, yet only a small amount of genetically modified foods that have caused drastic reactions in humans have been withdrawn. Where are the withdrawals from use in farm animals and pets? Did the crops get thrown away, buried, or burned, or did they sell the stuff to pet food manufacturers at reduced prices? The truth may never be known.

These allergy-causing crops induce inflammation throughout the body, which can lead to all kinds of diseases. The allergies then lead to the use of steroids and antibiotics in pets. This "standard of care" practice kills the flora in the gastrointestinal tract, which disables an immune system that has already been compromised by the use of steroids. A disabled immune system opens us—and our pets—up to many diseases, including cancer. Approximately one out of two pets dies of cancer. The other one dies of diabetes, heart disease, liver disease, kidney disease, etc.

One of the problematic GM products is an enzyme called barnase. Barnase is a known toxin that causes kidney damage and is in every cell of the canola plant.

The canola plant oil is in an abundance of pet foods, and it should not be. Monsanto makes a GM high-lysine corn. Along with the increased lysine from this corn, our pets are getting an increase in lysine by-products, one of them being saccharopine, at a level of fifty times that found in normal corn. The results of this and other lysine by-product consumption has not been tested or evaluated. Our dogs and cats are carnivores—not CORNivores!

This overdose of lysine, in combination with sugars and carbohydrates, along with the protein in corn when heated, causes a browning, taste-enhancing, and aroma-enhancing chemical reaction called a Maillard reaction. This chemical reaction occurs when amino acids are cooked in the presence of carbohydrates (exactly the recipe for baking or extrusion of dry pet food). This is a toxic reaction.

This reaction produces a compound known as AGEs, or advanced-glycation end products, that are linked with cancer, enhanced cancer progression, diabetes, kidney disease, neurodegenerative disease, dementia, Alzheimer's disease, decreased healing time, cataracts, and physical aging.

Notice that under the guaranteed analysis required by AAFCO, there is moisture, protein, fat, and fiber listed, but no carbohydrate requirement. Why? Because who would buy a bag, box, or can of pet food that has 50 percent cheap carbs listed in the ingredients? So let's not tell anybody and just leave this piece of incredible, valuable information off the label so everyone will be dumb and happy. The garbage will keep selling and the money will keep rolling in to the companies and their stockholders. But what about the animals? Who cares? They will get sick and everyone will make more money on sick care, and then you can just get another "replacement pet." Now that's a real advancement in veterinary medicine, isn't it?

Your dogs and cats are not carbivores—they are carnivores.

What about KMR (kitten milk replacer) and PMR (puppy milk replacer)? What are they made of? Formula is not mother's milk. Liberty Link crops marketed by Bayer Crop Science are tolerant to the Liberty herbicide glufosinate-ammonium. Liberty kills a wide variety of plants and can also kill bacteria, fungi, and insects. It is toxic to humans and animals. Glufosinate is structurally similar to a natural (found in nature) amino acid called glutamic acid, which can stimulate nerve cells to the point of death if enough is consumed. This glutamic acid is also found as the base for monosodium glutamate, otherwise known as MSG. As we all know, this "natural flavoring" is in vast amounts of food and can have many effects on the mood swings of people.

The tendency to fall asleep of one person and the hyper-activity of another, coupled with their inability to focus and concentrate, were observed by me from early childhood in Catholic elementary school. At that age, combined with my lack of experience in life, I could not distinguish whether I (and the other "kids") were going crazy from the MSG-laden soup that we were consuming or from the constant pressure of the nuns. Now, after almost seventy years later, I can assure you and myself that my childhood insanity was definitely due to combination of both.

The fact that glufosinate-induced kidney disease, respiratory distress, unconsciousness, and convulsions can be diagnosed in humans and not in pets is probably because of the level and expense of testing. Most of the time epilepsy, as well as the other conditions, are treated symptomatically and the root cause is not known (i.e., the definition of epilepsy). Again and again, the root cause comes from ingesting a varying level of a toxic substance or substances by way of the food.

Glufosinate is toxic to the gut bacteria, as are antibiotics. If you harm the gut, you harm the immune system. If you make the gut sick, you will make the immune system sick. The more you sicken the gut, the more destruction you cause to the immune system. After you have damaged or destroyed your immune system—as well as your pet's immune system—by the ingestion of toxic substances, you get a chronic—sometimes deadly—disease. The chronic, deadly disease may cost you hundreds of thousands—maybe millions—of dollars to stay alive.

The difference between you and your pet is that you have insurance mostly paid for through your employment. If you don't have great insurance, you are probably toast! However, I haven't seen or heard of anyone in over forty-seven years that has spent $100,000 on their pet, including insurance or not. The costs of MRIs, CAT scans, PET scans, x-rays, MUGA scans, sonograms and more sonograms, bone marrow transplants, organ transplants, extended hospitalization, intensive care, fluid therapy, chemotherapy, and radiation are prohibitive to most people regarding veterinary medicine.

And then there are the doctors upon doctors, with their specialized and sub-specialized knowledge and experience, along with their super-specialized consultation fees. These are also not feasible, doable, or payable in the normal scope of veterinary medicine, compromising the ability of the average animal doctor to diagnose and treat and the ability of the "pet parent" to pay. Our great-grandparents (and our grandparents) did not have anywhere near these problems with their pets because they shared wholesome table food and leftovers, unadulterated fresh foods, and canned foods preserved in glass jars, and their animal companions lived for extended periods of time without their human parents being financially strapped.

My great-grandparents were born in one-room thatched cottages in Ireland and had socio-political problems of their own. My great-grandfather was born John S. Broderick, of County Mayo, in the year 1840. That year was five years before the beginning of An Gorta Mor, or the Great Famine.

During An Gorta Mor, one third of the population of Ireland starved to death. It was called the Potato Famine because a potato parasite caused the potato crops to fail. Potatoes were supposedly the mainstay of the Irish people, and when the crops failed, there was nothing for the Irish to eat. If that story were true, then why were countless records kept of the many ships that sailed from Ireland to England, loaded with Irish cattle, Irish hogs, Irish chickens, and Irish sheep, all made of Irish protein and Irish fat? That does not sound like a relief effort for the Irish, does it? It sounds like genocide to me. Nutritional genocide! However, being Irish, they died sharing what little food they had with their pets. That, my friends, is unconditional love.

John Broderick survived An Gorta Mor and sailed to America in his early teens and died at age seventy-six in 1916, becoming the oldest living coastal freighter sea captain in New York harbor. My grandfather, Edward Francis Broderick Sr., the son of John S. Broderick, was born in 1882 in New York City and was a New York City fireman. He had a dog named Skippy, who lived to the age of twenty-three. Skippy never ate dog food or GM food because there wasn't any. Skippy ate what my grandparents ate. I never heard a story of Skippy being sick, and I never observed Skippy being sick.

Guess why he lived so long? Because he was never sick! Hello?? All my grandfather's friends had a dog and all of my grandmother's friends had cats. They all lived long into their twenties. They never ate pet food and there were certainly no GMOs! Grandma's cat lived till the age of twenty-five. Twenty-three plus twenty-five…I don't even need a calculator to come up with an average age of twenty-four for the cat and dog combination. And now we're down to around eight? That is only one-third of the pre-WWII lifespan of the cat and dog. That is an average of two-thirds of a lifespan lost in my seventy-four and a half years. What happened?

**ENTER THE EXTRUDER.**

# CHAPTER TEN

## The Extruder:
## The Goose that Laid Golden Eggs…
## For the Pet Food Cartel Anyway

IN THE EARLY 1950S, A MACHINE CALLED THE EXTRUDER was invented to cook and manufacture dry pet food, and it was at that time the pet food industry went into high gear. Extrusion made it possible to process the waste products of the fat-rendering industry. Rendering is when you take dead, down (disabled), diseased, and dying (4D) animals, including road kill, and boil them in a giant cauldron until

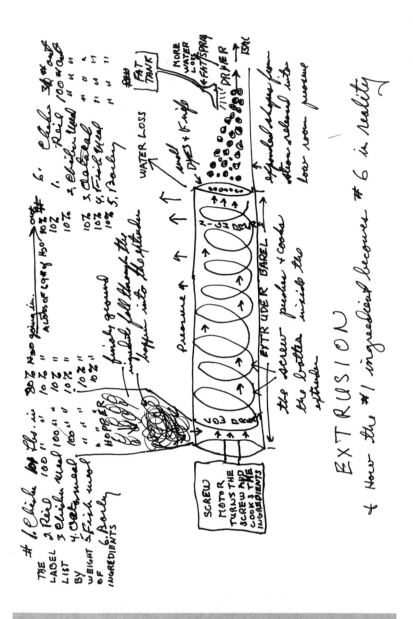

*The process of extruding pet food is complicated and often relies on substandard food. Illustration Credit: Doc Broderick*

the fat separates from the meat and bones and floats to the top of the vat. This rendered fat is skimmed off and sold as various categories of grease for frying, baking, and candlestick making, etc. The heavier meat and bones sink to the bottom of the tank, thus the name for the most undesirable parts of the animal is called "tankage."

This residue of rendering was dried and ground into different grades of meat and bone meal. The "meal," a finely ground, granular substance, is then packed in large bags or sold in bulk. At first, it was primarily used for hog and cattle feed or fertilizer. Now it is primarily used for pet food. The bone meal may contain aluminum cans, soda bottles, plastic bottles and bags, paper and plastic packaging, metal jar tops—all ground so finely that the added contaminants blend in and are undetectable by the naked eye. The meal may also contain antibiotics and steroid residues from the 4D animals as well as the GMOs they were fed or injected with, such as recombinant bovine growth hormone. This meal is now ready for the extruder to make expanded pet food.

The animal meal is mixed with corn meal, soybean meal, oatmeal, alfalfa meal, and corn distillers dried meal, a by-product of the liquor industry. Also added is bakery by-products meal (from the baking and candy industry,) which is loaded with sugar and flour, muffins, cakes, cookies, candies, chocolate, icing and fillers, along with any other ingredient that is swept or vacuumed off the processing equipment or floor.

This is then bagged or dumped into drums and loaded onto tractor trailers for delivery to the pet food factory, where it is incorporated as a profitable ingredient instead of being a costly liability that would have to be delivered to the local landfill or garbage dump for an expensive disposal fee.

Now you know why so many pet food companies are owned by conglomerates that make candy. This gives the mix about an average of 50 percent carbohydrates in the completed product. The carbs allow the mix to hold together and expand when they come out of the cannon barrel of the extruder.

Inside the extruder, there is a large steel screw turning at high speeds that "smooshes" the dough (which is made through steam injection into the meal) against the inner wall of the cannon barrel. This constant rubbing between the screw and the inner barrel wall cooks the dough in a process called *shear*. This is similar to rubbing your hands together to create an almost burning heat that not only dextronizes the starches in the sugar and carbs but creates a Maillard reaction that browns the dough as it passes through to the exit of the gun barrel.

This process causes a huge increase in pressure in the barrel. When the dough is pushed through the dies that form the shape of the finished product at the end of the barrel, the dough hits the low atmospheric (room) pressure and expands to form the shape of the finished product. Knives spinning at the end of the barrel cut the pieces to the desired length. Therefore, depending on the die and the speed of the knife, you can produce an expanded piece of dough to look like a circle, a square, any size of a pea, a nugget, a triangle, a star or a Cheerio, etc. Then the pieces fall on a belt and go through a dryer with high heat, producing even more of a Maillard reaction by baking the pieces.

This again adds to the problem caused by GMOs and enhances the potential carcinogenicity of the food. Roundup, which is the product name of glyphosate, is highly toxic. It can lead to a risk of cancer, reduced endocrine function, Parkinson's disease, lymphoma, miscarriages, and reduced semen quality, causing adverse effects on breeding, conception, and reproduction of all species. This goes against every basic law of nature. The FDA as well as the USDA continues to ignore the warnings and advice of the independent (not working for the biotech companies) scientific community, which continues to oppose the use of GMOs. Who is looking out for whom and, worse, why are they protecting industry instead of us and our families, including our pets?

GMO studies indicate that novel, foreign, untested genes have been put into our bodies and the bodies of our human children and pet children. These GM genes could create conditions in our bodies that are different from the way they were made to be over millions of years of evolution. We do not know anything about their long-term effects. What we do know is that a very small group of people are making billions of dollars by using us as guinea pigs. "Us" includes our pets, whose lifespan has already been decreased by one-half to two-thirds in my lifetime.

Our bodies and those of our pets act the same. The animal body receiving a foreign protein could see the protein as an unnatural and foreign invading substance. This causes an alarm to the immune (defense) system, which has more military personnel (immune cells) in our bodies and our pets' bodies than all the soldiers, sailors, coast guard, marines, and air force personnel from every country in the world combined!

These billions of cells can react slowly and insidiously, causing allergies and chronic, debilitating diseases. They may cause a rash equivalent to one bee sting with redness, swelling, heat, pain, and temporary loss of function—the definition of inflammation. Or the response could be violent, aggressive, and overwhelming (anaphylactic) and cause sudden death. Organic food by definition cannot contain GMOs. Organic food is our path to the survival of our human children as well as our pet children.

So next time you're in the grocery store or pet food shop looking for a can or bag of pet food, take a few minutes to start reading the labels and really learn what's in the food you're giving your animal, then you too, can start your pet down the road to a longer, healthier life, if you choose organic.

For more information on how to save everyone in your family from genetic modification, you must read the following books: Seeds of Deception and Genetic Roulette by Jeffrey M. Smith and also Altered Genes, Twisted Truth by Steven M. Druker. These are the references that I have read to formulate this chapter. They are a must-read for all of us.

## CHAPTER ELEVEN

# What Is the Cost to Have a Pet?

LET'S THINK ABOUT THIS FOR A MOMENT. WHAT WE'RE really asking is, what does it cost to have the luxury and the unbelievable experience of having a member of your family who gives you unconditional love 24/7 for their entire lifetime? The only cost you really have is food. Doesn't it seem fair that, for all they give us, they deserve to get at least equal quality food as the rest of the family?

What do we spend on the rest of our family on a daily basis that our pets never get? They never ask us for:

- Dancing lessons
- Singing lessons
- Music lessons
- Riding lessons
- Gymnastics lessons
- Soccer lessons
- Swimming lessons
- Spinning, Pilates, Zumba, and yoga classes
- Tutoring lessons
- Gym fees
- Tennis lessons
- Golf lessons
- Weddings
- Bar/Bat Mitzvahs
- Quinceanera celebrations
- Graduations with all the hoopla

Our pets don't have coaches or mentors. They don't go to events, concerts, or even a movie. They don't go shopping...ever! They don't go on vacations at home or abroad. They don't drink, smoke, talk back, text with cell phones requiring monthly expenses, or ask for the car keys. They are never rude and they don't EVER lie. There is no:

- Pre-K
- Kindergarten
- School, public or private

Nor is there college tuition and all the expenses that surround the constant travel (educational and social) activities that go on for at least the lifespan of any pet.

So when you are sipping your five-dollar latte treat as you drive around burning gallons of gas, think of the pennies on the dollar it costs you to thank the only one who gives you UNCONDITIONAL LOVE.

When I ask everyone (and I mean, I do ask everyone), "Do you and your two-legged children eat dog food?" Their response is always "No! God no! Are you kidding?" or, "Ewwwww!"

If it's that bad, I ask, "Why do you feed it to your pets? Why don't you feed your pets table scraps?" The answer is a resounding, "No, that's bad for the animals! I never feed anything but pet food because I was told all my life not to do that from every veterinarian that I have ever been to since I was eight years old."

Congratulations to all of us and our profession, who have slaughtered the Hippocratic Oath and programmed clients to do harm. Through our ignorance, inexperience, and naiveté as childhood students we listened to the lies and greed of the "experts" in the pet food cartel, who perpetrated these false and vicious stories about nutritious table food that our own mothers fed us—but led us to believe that it was not good for our pets! Then we perpetuated this blatant, damaging, and heartfelt deception to our clients using our clout as doctors—doctors who never designed or made pet food, doctors who never visited a pet food factory and, if they had once, they went home, showered, and never went back. But, most of all, we let down and compromised the animals we swore to protect from harm.

And on a personal level, we let ourselves down by compromising the dream we had as little children. For whatever reason, our dream was simply to help those beloved creatures that walked us to school and cuddled with us at night and kept us warm. They took the fear of life away from us and gave us security and sanity in the face of what appeared to be, at times, an insane world.

We wanted to be like them—the purest form of all God's children. They are the ones who caused us to become animal doctors.

Join me, please, in ending the lies and giving them the opportunity to have the food that THEY too deserve.

# EPILOGUE

SINCE I LEFT THE CLASS OF DR. RUSSELL FREY AND GRADU-ated from veterinary medical school, I had three objectives in mind: First, to be the finest veterinary surgeon that I could be without doing harm. Second, to be a good doctor without pushing drugs. The third was to be a great teacher—not a teacher of the magnitude of Upson and Frey, but one who could spend his life trying to come as close as I could to these heroes of knowledge and personal communication.

If I could tell the world, one person at a time, how to feed their animals, I could double their pet's lifespan back to where it was when I was born. If I also could make the supreme food for pets, I could guarantee my dream would endure. That struggle has been a more than forty-seven-year work-in-progress that not only is working, but that defies the naysayers. It is ever-growing and dynamic. It is wholesome, nourishing in its contents, and hopeful and healing in its scope. It is not the best, because the next batch and truckload will be better and better after that. It has set the standard for every pet food out there since we started, and it will continue as long as my name is on it and my passion is behind it. I have talked the talk but you must listen, and then if you walk the walk with me, together we will make this non-toxic, real, beyond organic, and supreme Paradigm defy all odds and return our animal children to a long life of vibrant health. I know your pets will thank and love you for it.

**God bless you and your beloved pets,**

**Dr. Geoff Broderick**

# ABOUT THE AUTHOR

- Born October 23, 1941 in New York City to Irish/German first-generation American parents

- 1950s – Rodeo cowboy, black diamond wild west show cast member

- 1958-59 – Member of 82ND Airborne Division, paratrooper U.S. Army; '60-'61 – 7TH Infantry Division, Korea

- 1961 – Age 19, attended Embry-Riddle Aeronautical University for advanced pilot training

- 1962 – Attended Delhi A&T College, first class of veterinary technicians in the U.S.

- 1963-69 – Kansas State University, Bachelor of Science, Doctor of Veterinary Medicine

- 1969 – Opened Southdown Animal Clinic, Huntington, NY

- 1970-1990s – International polo player for twenty years, Captain Team Cornucopia; winner of the World Ambassadors Cup: Team Central America

- 1970s – Speaker: declared the national movement against sugar and chemicals in pet food at the Health and Nutrition Expo in New York City; this was the official start of the Natural Pet Food Movement in America

- 1975 – Developer and manufacturer of Cornucopia Natural Pet Food

- 1977 – Journalist of Radio Free Europe and The Voice of America, Ben Grauer introduced Dr. Broderick on his final career broadcast as "The American Dream"

- March 1978 – Award from Committee for World Health for his pioneering work with vitamin C, presented scientific paper: Cure,

Prevention, and Control of Cystitis and Urinary Tract and Infection by Oral Administration of Ascorbic Acid

- 1978 – Developed the first pet food to provide proper pH of urine to prevent struvite (triple phosphate) urinary stones

- 1979 – Formulated and manufactured Cornucopia Super-Food and Phyto-Food

- 1980 – Award recipient, California Orthomolecular Medical Society presented scientific paper, dissolved the first urinary stone without surgical intervention

- 1983 – Doc produced the food for President Reagan to relieve the famine in Ethiopa

- 1983 – Developed and manufactured the first extruded horse food for the prevention of the five major diseases of the horse

- January 25, 1990 – one of the first three doctors who responded to the site of the Avianca Flight 52 Columbian airplane disaster

- 1997 – Calcutta, India, met with Mother Teresa several times. He received messages from her for the animals of the world

- August 2012 – At the American Veterinary Convention in San Diego, California, Dr. Geoffrey Broderick received the first President's Award in Veterinary Medicine

- Dr. Broderick is in his 48[TH] year of veterinary medical practice at his Animal Clinic at Southdown in Huntington, NY 11743 and is still creating Supreme Nutrition for Pets as the CEO of Cornucopia Pet Foods.

To contact Dr. Geoffrey Broderick

or Cornucopia Pet Foods

Please visit our website at:

www.cornucopiapetfoods.com

or email us at:

info@cornucopiapetfoods.com

*or*

Cornucopia Pet Foods, Ltd.

229 Wall Street | Huntington, NY 11743

*or*

Pet Health Line:

1-800-PET-8280 or 631-427-7479

or

Fuhgeddaboudit!

CPSIA information can be obtained at www.ICGtesting.com
Printed in the USA
BVOW02*1702240716

456545BV00001B/1/P